HOSTILE TAKEOVER

Studies in American Political Institutions and Public Policy
General Editor: James W. Ceaser, University of Virginia

Presenting works on contemporary American politics that address the question of how institutions and policies can best function to sustain a healthy liberal democratic government in the United States.

Congress' Permanent Minority? Republicans in the U.S. House
by William F. Connelly, Jr., and John J. Pitney, Jr.

Hostile Takeover: The House Republican Party, 1980–1995
by Douglas L. Koopman

HOSTILE TAKEOVER

The House Republican Party, 1980–1995

Douglas L. Koopman

ROWMAN & LITTLEFIELD PUBLISHERS, INC.

ROWMAN & LITTLEFIELD PUBLISHERS, INC.

Published in the United States of America
by Rowman & Littlefield Publishers, Inc.
4720 Boston Way, Lanham, Maryland 20706

3 Henrietta Street
London WC2E 8LU, England

British Cataloging in Publication Information Available

Library of Congress Cataloging-in-Publication Data
Koopman, Douglas L.
Hostile takeover : the House Republican Party, 1980–1995 / by
Douglas L. Koopman.
p.   cm. — (Studies in American political institutions and
public policy)
Includes bibliographical references and index.
1. Republican Party (U.S. : 1854–   ).   2. United States.   Congress.
House.   3. United States—Politics and government—1981-1989.
4. United States—Politics and government—1989–   I. Title.
II. Series.
JK1319.K66   1996   324.2734'09'048—dc20   96-435   CIP

ISBN 0–8476–8168–8 (cloth : alk. paper)
ISBN 0–8476–8169–6 (pbk : alk. paper)

Printed in the United States of America

∞ ™ The paper used in this publication meets the minimum requirements of
American National Standard for Information Sciences—Permanence of
Paper for Printed Library Materials, ANSI Z39.48–1984.

Contents

v

Tables

Introduction

Studying the House Republican Party

Political scientists have long studied the U.S. House of Representatives, and there is now almost an embarrassment of riches in most areas of congressional and legislative studies. Congress is an open environment, with staff and members frequently eager to speak with interested researchers. Congress, especially the House of Representatives, produces and requires the paperwork and documentation that are great resources for scholars. There are hundreds of roll-call votes each Congress that can undergo complex statistical analysis. Research on voting patterns has been especially attractive since the mid-1970s, when electronic voting increased the number of recorded votes. Information on campaign funds is plentiful, especially since the 1970s campaign legislation required much fuller candidate, party, and contributor disclosure.

Yet at least one area remains virtually unexplored—the minority (almost always Republican) party in the House. There are studies of party leaders, but most focus on the majority-party leadership. In studies of congressional-presidential relations, the congressional side is dominated by the images of majority party leaders. There are also studies of the relationship of House leaders to rank-and-file members, but most focus on relations in the majority. Committee studies are numerous, but few mention the role of partisanship in committee deliberations or wonder how that role has changed.

There are at least two possible reasons for the neglect of the minority. First, because the minority party holds no committee chairs and only secondarily important party positions, many scholars regard the minority party as an insignificant player. Partisan identification may also play a role. The minority party in the House from 1954 through 1994 was the Republican party, and for at least thirty years

1

before that its majority status was narrow and infrequent. Most political scientists, especially at major research universities, identify themselves as moderates or liberals, and Democrats. Thus, the second reason may be that most researchers are likely to have contacts on the Democratic side of the aisle, which leads to access, interviews, and research projects focused on that party.[1]

This neglect has not always existed, and there are a few comprehensive treatments of the House minority party. Charles O. Jones's 1965 book, *Party and Policy-Making: The House Republican Policy Committee,*[2] studied the origin and development of the House Republican Policy Committee, observed its contributions to policy development and partisan unity, and made recommendations to improve House Republican policy-making. Jones's second work, *The Minority Party in Congress*, was written in 1970.[3] It was the only book-length study in nearly twenty-five years whose primary focus was the Republican party in the House of Representatives. Jones sought to describe the context of minority-party decision making. He identified various external and internal influences on the ability of the minority congressional party to present an alternative policy platform. These conditions combined in different ways from Congress to Congress to empower or constrain Republicans. Jones also identified the strategies that an organized congressional opposition could adopt. While much of Jones's perceptive model still holds, much has happened to the minority party in the last twenty-five years. The subject needs reexamination, especially the institutional context.

Since Jones's 1970 work, only a few authors have looked at the Republican party in the House, and then almost always as a vehicle to describe GOP changes outside the institution. A. James Reichley, in his 1981 *Conservatives in an Age of Change,*[4] studied the Nixon-Ford era, painting a picture of a four-faction GOP in both the electorate and the party elite. Including House Republicans in his analysis, Reichley made divisions according to ideological differences, what he called "tribal loyalties," and views on political strategy.

His four groups of Republicans were Fundamentalists, Stalwarts, Moderates, and Progressives, and his description of them was rich and detailed. Reichley categorized House Republicans into these four factions based upon *Congressional Quarterly*'s Conservative Coalition scores. Fundamentalists most often supported the coalition, with Stalwarts, Moderates, and Progressives, in order, voting less frequently in support of the Conservative Coalition.

Reichley's descriptions of each faction were thorough. Unfortunately, this richness of description has become less meaningful because it relied on Conservative Coalition scores. The Conservative Coalition shrank in significance in the contemporary era, as southern Democrats were replaced by Republicans or by Democrats similar to those from the rest of the nation, and as floor rules and Democratic leadership innovations muted intraparty divisions. In addition, Conservative Coalition scores are unidimensional, failing to distinguish among economic, social, and foreign policy conservatism. This limitation tends to group too many House members together in too few factions. Thus, when Reichley's categorization is applied to the 103rd Congress, nearly all Republicans fall into the Fundamentalist camp. While the House GOP has probably become more conservative in the last twenty years, it would be incorrect to state that nearly all House Republicans fit the Fundamentalist description.

Another effort to describe factions in the GOP was made by Nicol Rae in his mid-1980s *The Decline and Fall of Liberal Republicans*.[5] Like Reichley, Rae relied upon the decreasingly useful Conservative Coalition scores. The advantages of Rae's work, however, are that it gave a great deal of attention to congressional Republicans and looked beyond floor votes for factional cleavages. Rae discerned three different bases of intraparty GOP conflict: sectional (Sunbelt vs. Frostbelt), ideological (conservative vs. liberal), and attitudinal (purists vs. professional), the last division cutting across all ideological and sectional groups similar to that described in the 1960s by James Q. Wilson.[6] The intraparty disagreement here is not over which ideology to adopt, but more over *whether* to campaign openly on ideology.[7] Purists tend to use the party apparatus to pursue ideological agendas. Professionals support whatever type of nominee is offered, preferring nominees who are nonideological party regulars.

Despite the limitations of his roll-call-based analysis, Rae nevertheless made a large contribution by adding the purist/professional dimension to studies of intraparty conflict. This new dimension highlights the tensions raised by differing attitudes among party members.

These differences are expanded upon by Howard Reiter, who has developed a model of intraparty tension.[8] His model applies to both parties, but it is especially useful for a Republican party with a long history of fighting over the best strategy to gain a congressional majority. Reiter observed that American political parties generally have two ''clusters''—a Dominant cluster and a Minority cluster closer in policy positions to the other party. In the case of the GOP, the Minority cluster is more liberal. Under a stable minority party regime, both Minority and Dominant clusters perceive the same issues as salient. As new issues arise, the Dominant cluster splits into Regulars and Realigners. Regulars prefer to emphasize old issues in old ways. Realigners vote with the Regulars, but emphasize new issues to attract new members to the party.

Several characteristics set Realigners apart. They believe in issues and ideologies, think that the electorate can be issue oriented, and think the public will agree with the Realigners' side of these newly emphasized issues. Regulars, on the other hand, may prefer the *status quo* for a number of reasons. They may be from states where they are a majority, they may see the new issues as transitory, they might have misgivings about issue demagoguery, or they may even prefer controlling a minority over sharing power in a majority.

The previous Minority faction of the party could be relabeled, in the new context, Misfits. Regulars still accept these Misfits, but Realigners might seek to drive them out in order to make the party more attractive to new groups.

Reiter expected Regulars and Misfits to reside in areas of traditional party strength. Misfits might be especially prevalent in traditional areas because they have had little incentive to join the party recently. Realigners, on the other hand, would appear in areas of new party strength. Misfits and Realigners would tend to have organizational groups outside the formal party apparatus; Regulars would already control the nominal party levers.

Reiter's model conforms nicely to recent Republican history. GOP Regulars are embodied by Gerald Ford in the late 1960s and 1970s and George Bush in the late 1970s through the present. Misfits are, of course, liberal Republicans such as Nelson Rockefeller, Charles Mathias, and Lowell Weicker. GOP Realigners come from the Sunbelt, Regulars from the Midwest, and Misfits from the Northeast. Realigners in Congress organized the Republican Study Committee and Conservative Opportunity Society, Misfits had the Ripon Society, and Regulars have until recently held most House party offices. In the last few years, however, the Realigners have captured most House GOP party leadership offices after slowly emerging as the dominant faction, or actually pair of factions, in the party.

Although not strictly a study of House Republicans, Reiter's study deserves mention because of its application to changes in the House GOP the last decade and more. A minor concern with Reiter's analysis is how it was applied to the present Republican party. He labeled the Goldwater-Reagan element of the GOP as the sole Realigning element within the Republican party. But disagreement within this group over social issues suggest there is more than one Realigning group.

A more detailed portrayal of new conservative influences in American politics has been completed by Paul Gottfried and Thomas Fleming.[9] Briefly, they find four new conservative influences that have strongly affected the Republican party—the religious right, a populist "New Right," libertarians, and neoconservatives. The religious right has been the largest new source of public followers, and neoconservatives have had the most intellectual weight. Populist New Right activists and libertarians have also come to the GOP. All four elements, especially the populist and religious groups, fed the anti-establishment sentiment Ronald Reagan fostered in 1980, a feeling House Republicans counted on for numerical gains in the Reagan years.

These four groups have brought two policy dimensions to the GOP. The first is a conservative religious agenda with roots in the religious right but orchestrated by both religious right and some New Right activists. The second dimension is a new approach to domestic needs finding intellectual backing in part of the neoconservative movement. While there are areas of agreement, the two policy dimensions do clash over, for example, how much to emphasize conservative social issues. This tension may well intensify now that the House GOP has gained majority status.

Congress' Permanent Minority?,[10] by William F. Connelly, Jr., and John J. Pitney, Jr., is the first work in many years that examines House Republicans. It reviews the recent history of the House from the GOP perspective and explains some of the challenges facing the House party in the mid-1990s. These authors point out that the apparent unity of House floor voting is largely a product of an intensely partisan House. In the post-reform era, floor rules, oversight responsibilities, legislative initiatives, campaign finances, committee staff, and individual perquisites were all used by the Democratic majority in a manner perceived by Republicans as highly partisan. As Republicans of all stripes saw themselves treated unfairly by the Democratic majority, they joined more reliably in united opposition. Thus, as these authors mention, the hostility of the 1980s and early 1990s partially masked the ideological, strategic, generational, and other differences that distinguish groups of House Republicans from each other. Now that the partisan context has changed, GOP fissures may become more apparent.

The Connelly/Pitney book is an important beginning in understanding the House Republicans. It is really a reintroduction to the study of

House Republicans and an argument for greater attention to two issues—recent changes within the House Republican party, and disagreements between the two major parties in the operation of our national legislature. Although written before Republicans gained majority status, most of its insights still apply.

The work presented here is an attempt to advance the understanding of these two critical issues. It is written for two major reasons. The first reason is to help cultivate that spot in the field of congressional research that remains largely undisturbed. Careful study of House partisanship and minority party strategies can produce fruitful information and nourish additional research projects. In the aftermath of the 1994 elections, such research can shed light on how a congressional minority party essentially shut out of the legislative process could still nationalize an election into a referendum on a specific policy agenda. The major focus of this work is the changing institutional circumstances that encouraged House Republicans to move from a passive opposition accepting permanent minority status to an activist opposition, and ultimately to a majority.

The second reason for undertaking this work is more personal. I found little connection between the House described in the academic literature and the House that I have observed since 1980. While most scholars saw a decentralized House with junior entrepreneurial members making creative contributions, I witnessed a growing centralization that excluded many members (of both parties) with creative policy approaches. While reading about the decline of partisanship, I saw majority-party leaders limiting minority-party participation and virtually shutting out all Republican members. As most commentators saw an increasingly homogeneous and conservative House GOP Conference, I observed fights over issues, tactics, and leaders, usually conducted by leaders of several party "factions"—many of which were won by moderates. Finally, while the literature talked about the growing "localization" of member activities to serve constituents, many minority-party members were pursuing party-building strategies. In brief, the literature did not match experience. While observations can be skewed, it seemed that much of the story about the House in the post-reform era and the role of the Republican party in it needed to be told.

In examining the House Republicans from the 1980s to the present, this work traces the recent history of old and new conservative movements and their relationship to the Republican party. Conservative movements are more complex than usually realized. This study identifies different strains of conservative thought and how they relate to House GOP factions. It also analyzes the relative stability and size of these factions. In doing so, it develops a model of intraparty factionalism.

This work examines the claims by House Republicans that the House has become far more partisan. It looks at procedural, committee, and electoral data, to detect trends and partisan differences developing in the post-reform era. It also critiques some of the research that assumes much of the House's business takes place by nonpartisan or bipartisan agreement.

The book relies more on data than anecdotes. The approach is intentional, for many times Republican complaints have been dismissed as stemming from incidental events that do not indicate any pattern of unfairness.[11] While not accepting Republican complaints at face value, this analysis carefully weighs Republican claims about the partisanship and unfairness in the post-reform House.

The work attempts to make an early contribution to renewed study of the Republican party in the U.S. House of Representatives. It covers the transformation of a minority GOP from muted opposition to aggressive partisanship, forced upon Republicans (in the minds of many of them) by unfair Democratic party tactics hostile to the chamber's deliberative purpose. This transformation was gradual and controversial, but the evolving constellation of factions illustrates the pace and direction of change, and the inevitable success of GOP activists. This takeover was not always peaceful; hence, the title of this work also refers to a frequent attribute of the aggressive conservative takeover of the House GOP—hostility to less assertive colleagues. In addition, the work describes how the ultimately successful aggressive partisanship shaped the 1994 election strategy that gave Republicans a House majority for the first time in forty years.

While the focus is on the GOP, the study also has relevance to larger issues of congressional reform and partisanship. A House majority party may resist calls for reform, but eventually the weaknesses of the old ways will become more obvious and a skillful minority party may make institutional change a winning election issue. While a strong majority-party leadership may keep its party members together and shun the minority, it does so at the risk of alienating too much of the electorate and being portrayed as out of touch with mainstream public opinion. If there is one lesson of the post-reform era, it is that there are limits to partisanship within the House of Representatives. The

Democrats learned it the hard way and Republicans would do well to remember it.

The final contribution of this work is to develop new explanations of intraparty conflict. The House Republican party transformed itself into an aggressive minority party and then took control of the House. The numerous factions in the House GOP were muted in minority status, and for a time it may be that Republicans will remain united. Over time, however, that unity may dissolve. A narrow GOP majority may face repeated frustration, as anything less than unanimity means party defeat. Majorities will be made too forcefully, frustrating one or more factions in the party, or the party will fail, frustrating the leadership. Alternatively, a larger GOP majority may encourage some party factions to distinguish themselves from the new party mainstream. Either way, the factions described here may well foreshadow future conflicts within the Congress and among Republicans, whether or not they retain their position as the new congressional majority.

Notes

1. See, for example, Walter B. Roettger and Hugh Winebrenner, "Politics and Political Scientists," *Public Opinion* 9 (September/October 1986): 41–44, and Roettger and Winebrenner, "The Voting Behavior of American Political Scientists: The 1980 Presidential Election," *Western Political Quarterly* 36 (1983): 134–48.

2. Charles O. Jones, *Party and Policy-Making: The House Republican Policy Committee* (New Brunswick, N.J.: Rutgers University Press, 1965).

3. Charles O. Jones, *The Minority Party in Congress* (Boston: Little, Brown, 1970).

4. A. James Reichley, *Conservatives in an Age of Change: The Nixon and Ford Administrations* (Washington, D.C.: Brookings Institution, 1981).

5. Nicol Rae, *The Decline and Fall of Liberal Republicans: 1952 to the Present* (New York: Oxford University Press, 1989).

6. James Q. Wilson, *The Amateur Democrat* (Chicago: University of Chicago Press, 1966).

7. Rae, 6.

8. Howard Reiter, "Intra-Party Cleavages in the United States Today," *Western Political Quarterly* 34 (1981): 287–300 passim.

9. Paul Gottfried and Thomas Fleming, *The Conservative Movement* (Boston: Twayne Publishers, 1988).

10. William F. Connelly, Jr., and John J. Pitney, Jr. *Congress' Permanent Minority?: Republicans in the U.S. House* (Lanham, Md.: Rowman & Littlefield, 1994).

11. For a good description of Democratic thinking on this issue see David W. Rohde, *Parties and Leaders in the Postreform House* (Chicago: University of Chicago Press, 1991), especially chapters 4, "The Democratic Leadership: Party Agents and Agenda Management" and 6, "Conclusions and Future Prospects." This work is also the first to begin to take seriously Republican complaints of increased partisanship, in chapter 5, "Republican Reactions, Presidential Agendas, and Legislative Consequences."

Chapter 1

Changing GOP Leadership: Gingrich vs. Madigan in 1989

On Friday, March 10, 1989, at 10:00 a.m., President George Bush announced he would nominate Representative Richard B. Cheney of Wyoming, the House Republican Whip, to be secretary of defense (the president's first nominee, John Tower, had just been rejected by the U.S. Senate). By 11:00 a.m., Representative Newt Gingrich of Georgia, who held no House leadership position, announced that he would seek the Whip vacancy created by Cheney's resignation. The next Wednesday Gingrich claimed he had seventy-two votes in the 174-member House Republican Conference, a long way toward the majority needed to win the post.[1] Seven days later, March 22, House Republicans narrowly elected Gingrich their new Whip, eighty-seven to eighty-five, with two members not voting. Gingrich's opponent had been Ed Madigan of Illinois, who had been Chief Deputy GOP Whip for Cheney and for Cheney's predecessor Trent Lott. He had also chaired the Republican Research Committee and followed the traditional conciliatory leadership style of House Republican Leader Robert Michel.[2]

Gingrich was the first announced Whip candidate, but he was not the early favorite. In fact, behind the scenes there was an almost frantic search to find an opponent who could keep Gingrich off the leadership ladder. Jerry Lewis of California, recently elected Republican conference chairman (the number-three position), was mentioned most often as the alternative. Lewis had won close victories in other tough leadership battles. Said one GOP aide on March 12, "if you have to bet five bucks today, you've got to bet on Lewis."[3] Vin Weber of Minnesota, Bill McCollum of Florida, and Mickey Edwards of Oklahoma, all members of the leadership, also were possible candidates. From the leadership perspective, each of these alternatives had the advantage of some connection to younger and more activist House Republicans, yet each was easier to work with than the volatile Gingrich. But none seriously explored candidacies, and Lewis soon backed off at Michel's behest in order to consolidate anti-Gingrich forces around Madigan.[4]

The March 1989 House Republican Whip race differed from most leadership races within the minority party.[5] Such races are usually low-profile contests held after November elections when media attention is reviewing election results or slowing down for the holidays. One difference in this case was public attention. The obvious reason was the involvement of Gingrich, an aggressive and articulate Republican who was pressuring the House Committee on Standards of Official Conduct (Ethics) to investigate Speaker Jim Wright. And the unscheduled opening of the Whip position made it the only leadership race at the time, "the only game in town" for congressional reporters.

The Gingrich-Madigan Whip race also had important implications for future leadership of House Republicans. The House GOP in 1989 had just lost some of its key members, including Jack Kemp in a failed 1988 presidential primary campaign and Trent Lott in a successful Mississippi Senate bid. Cheney's pending departure removed the most likely heir to Republican Leader Michel. There was no obvious successor to the Illinoisan, who had entered the House in 1956, had been Leader since 1981, and who was mulling retirement. As a consequence, most of the media and many House Republicans viewed the winner of the Whip race as a likely future House Republican Leader.[6]

Lower-ranking House GOP leaders, however, historically had not ascended as regularly to the top spot as Democratic party leaders. This less regular GOP ascendancy resulted from the fact that the GOP had been in the minority most of the time there had been institutionalized House leadership. Rank-and-file legislators vent their frustration with minority status by changing their leadership.[7]

The two Whip candidates voiced widely divergent views on what was at stake. Madigan described the minority Whip as vote counter and coalition builder, and disavowed any interest in succeeding Michel. He thought the Whip must "help President Bush be an effective chief executive," and help with "getting things done."[8] "The Whip is the guy who makes things work. The job description is coalition-building,"[9] Madigan said. Madigan assured his colleagues he had no interest in succeeding Michel as Leader, believing this stated lack of ambition would be an argument in his favor.

Madigan had many assets. His style was conciliatory, and he had accomplished many things while abiding by the House's historic norms. He had a long legislative record, wielding influence on the Agriculture and Energy and Commerce committees. He also had many organizational strengths—the existing Whip structure of which he was second in command, senior members with whom he had long association, and members of the important committees where he was a ranking member.[10]

Gingrich's strategy was different. He argued that "the Whip's race is more important and decisive because it's a race about what we're going to become," about "what kind of party" the GOP would be. He described the race as a choice between the party's cooperative, "timid" manner of dealing with Democrats and the more assertive and even hostile style Gingrich had demonstrated since he entered Congress in 1978.[11] Gingrich wanted to overturn the mindset among the House GOP leadership: "getting the crumbs" given them by an unfair Democratic majority.[12] "If all we have to offer as Republicans is simply half of the corrupt liberal welfare state, that's crazy. There has to be fundamental reform."[13] To Gingrich, a Madigan win would doom Republicans but a Gingrich victory would mean a majoritarian GOP revolution in the House.[14] In contrast to Madigan, Gingrich barely hid his ambition to succeed Michel as Leader, freely admitting his desire to lead House Republicans from the top spot.

Gingrich had made little legislative impact as measured in terms of bills sponsored, cosponsored, or enacted.[15] Instead, he had concentrated on electoral and political considerations. Since 1986 until 1995, for example, he was leader of GOPAC, a political action committee funding and advising state and local GOP candidates. Gingrich and his cohorts in the Conservative Opportunity Society (COS) had also given birth to many new ideas, most outside of the legislative mainstream.

Gingrich soon had framed the press and pundits' views of the race's implications. Eddie Mahe, a Republican political operative, said "Newt's conception of the job is figuring out how to become a majority. Madigan's concept of the job is figuring out how to get along with Democrats."[16] Paul Gigot in the *Wall Street Journal* wrote "old bulls strive to be 'influential' with House Democrats, even when their only influence is to enhance the Democrats' agenda. Their conceit is that they help 'govern' when in fact they lose. Mr. Gingrich would rather play offense."[17] Wesley Pruden of the *Washington Times* wrote, "on one side are the kind of Republicans who think it's not nice to be rude to Democrats, and on the other are the Republicans who think it's rude to Republicans to be nice to Democrats."[18] He went on:

> The go-fers and towel boys are represented by Edward Madigan. . . . Gingrich is the candidate who could give new meaning to the word "whip." He might use it on the opposition, which makes him a favorite of neither Mr. Michel nor the Democratic leadership. . . . He gives certain other Republican heartburn, too. These are, by and large, the Republicans who are comfortable with their party's congressional role as the permanent opposition.[19]

A "Responsible" House Republican Party?

Gingrich expanded the meaning of the race beyond its traditional considerations. It joined a broader public debate on the appropriate role of a congressional minority party, in relation both to a congressional majority and to the president.

At one pole of this debate is the "responsible party" view expressed in, for example, the 1950 report *Toward a More Responsible Two-Party System,* written by a committee of the American Political Science Association (APSA).[20] This perspective holds that political parties should develop cohesive policy platforms, that elected officials should follow these policy guidelines, and that the party should employ sanctions against recalcitrant party members. Under this view, the minority congressional party must present a regular set of policy options different from the majority party. The congressional party's relationship to a president of its own party should, the report also asserts, be one of support, with the congressional party taking its lead from the president of its own party.

Two shortcomings of the APSA report are significant here. First, it did not dwell on the possibility of split party control of the national government. There is barely a mention of the role of a congressional minority party that also claims the presidency.

The second shortcoming is that the report overlooked the different electoral bases of presidents and lawmakers. James MacGregor Burns in *The Deadlock of Democracy*[21] and others have acknowledged electoral divisions between presidents and representatives, and usually proposed remedies, mostly impractical. Only recently have scholars tried to come to terms with the need for new political theorizing in an era of "coalition government."[22]

At the other pole of the debate is the argument that responsible parties have no place in the United States. This second view notes the impediments built into the constitutional and political order, and accepts the "irresponsibility" of American political parties. A prime example of this thinking is, of course, *Federalist 10*.[23]

These two positions can be labeled the "responsible" and "pragmatic" views. A third alternative is possible. It is conceivable to have "responsible" parties based in different institutions or levels of government. This view argues that a large measure of party responsibility is important and achievable. Responsibility can be based in government institutions—such as among party members in the House and Senate separately or together, in the executive—or at the various government levels in a federal system. Nominal party colleagues could disagree, as long as there was basic agreement *within* institutions or government levels and an agreement to disagree across institutions or levels.

This alternative builds on Burns's observation in *Deadlock of Democracy* that each party has a congressional/presidential split in issue emphasis and voter evaluation. Unlike Burns, however, this proposal accepts the split and posits a responsible and usually cooperative party in separate institutions. This view would allow House members to formulate a domestic agenda while letting the president focus on national security.

To the extent the role of party was an issue in 1989, Madigan backers held either to the responsible party model guided by presidential leadership, or the pragmatic belief that issue-based political parties were not important. Madigan's statements outlining his qualifications and his vision of the job suggest both possibilities. Gingrich and his backers argued that House Republicans should develop a more responsible and independent House GOP apparatus and issue agenda. Minnesota Republican Vin Weber, organizer of Gingrich's campaign, claimed House Republicans "can lead the White House, [which] will look to Congress for leadership on that whole second tier of issues that make up the domestic agenda."[24]

Political scientists commenting on the Gingrich-Madigan race generally reflected the dominant thinking of the responsible party model, even though the theory had not functioned well in the United States and would operate even less successfully under split control of the national government. Thomas Mann of the Brookings Institution said:

> if Gingrich gets in, it would be very bad for Bush. His highest priority would be in attacking Democrats and getting a Republican majority in the

House, not in getting Bush's agenda through the House. . . . [T]he only
hope of getting anything done was in working with Democrats . . . to deal
successfully with issues like the budget and child care.[25]

Norman Ornstein of the American Enterprise Institute argued the
same point, more thoroughly. He believed that electoral success depended upon one unified and policy-oriented party. He pointed out
that Republican presidential coattails no longer existed—landslides by
Reagan and Bush did little to usher Republicans into Congress. And
he accurately perceived that Gingrich was supported by Republicans
looking out for their own interests, specifically lower taxes, less
government, and greater attention to domestic issues required by
the House's more frequent and personal elections.[26] But he thought
Gingrich's election would be "trouble for Bush" even though low
taxes and less government composed most of the president's purported
domestic agenda, because Gingrich would not be willing to accept
compromises worked out by House Democratic leaders and President
Bush.

A few journalists thought that an aggressive House GOP might
enhance party fortunes. Richard E. Cohen, writing for the *National
Journal*, noted:

> Contrary to the skeptics' views, Gingrich's election poses challenges to
> both parties. Gingrich says his aggressive style can aid Republicans and
> the Bush Administration by helping them develop more appealing and
> better-defined policies. . . . [T]he conflict resulting from sharpened
> partisan lines, in turn, can help promote truly bipartisan and more
> effective solutions to national problems.[27]

The most plausible interpretation of the Gingrich victory follows
Cohen's reporting: a slim majority of House Republicans had signaled
a new strategy to gain majority status through a "responsible" congressional Republican party with a credible domestic policy agenda.
This positive domestic agenda would directly challenge House Democrats, and might at times even be hostile to a Republican president
(when there was one) and to resistant House GOP leaders. But new
leaders such as Gingrich would work toward that end. The five years
between 1989 and 1994 are essentially the story of how Gingrich and
like-minded leaders gradually persuaded enough House Republicans to
present a specific domestic agenda in congressional elections.

Intraparty Factions

The Gingrich-Madigan race was also different because it clearly illustrated House GOP factions[28] and the cross-cutting pressures between policy-oriented activists and constituency-oriented conformists.

Commentators had difficulty explaining why certain individuals or groups voted for one or the other candidate. A *Washington Post* report noted that Gingrich's majority was "a largely unknown army of younger conservatives who combined with some moderates, women and even a few of the old guard."[29] The report did not explain why young conservatives differed from old ones, why some moderates chose Gingrich over Madigan, what GOP women saw in Gingrich, and why some in the old guard broke with their peers.

The confusion of most commentators stemmed from the predominant method of identifying factions—roll-call vote analysis—and the predominant conclusion about House Republicans from that analysis— that all House Republicans (except for a dwindling group in the Northeast) are alike. Roll-call analysis cannot explore cleavages over the very things at issue in the Gingrich-Madigan race: tactics, norms, and party responsibility. The assumptions of roll-call research are that intraparty disagreement is restricted to policy options, and that this disagreement is measurable by roll-call analysis. Roll-call research does not leave room for factions that form over other matters—such as tactics, types of member activity, or personalities. Congressional commentary also rarely moves beyond classifying members as either liberals or conservatives. Anyone not fitting in this unidimensional world is a "moderate" or, if media-hungry, perhaps a "maverick."

Media analysis of the 1989 Whip race was blurry. The *Washington Post* reported, for example, that "conservative Republicans rejoiced at the outcome,"[30] even though a matching of ideological ratings and Whip vote results indicate no conservative triumph.[31] The average Conservative Coalition scores were 85.99 for Gingrich supporters and 83.52 for Madigan backers, and support for each candidate came from all points on the GOP ideological spectrum. Indeed, the most visible dissatisfaction with the old leadership came from the '92 Group, an informal caucus of approximately forty House GOP moderates and liberals. Yet '92 Group members voted for Gingrich by a three-to-one margin, according to the group's chair, New York Representative Sherwood Boehlert.[32]

Some reports were more precise in labeling the race as a clash between the GOP's "pragmatic" wing and a more partisan and confrontational faction.[33] The *National Journal* said that House Republicans were "voting to turn their party toward a more activist and confrontational style of leadership in the House."[34] Richard E. Cohen suggested that GOP moderates and liberals resented both Democratic tactics and GOP leadership acquiescence to them. These members, without much influence in the leadership, were receptive to anti-establishment strategies in order to gain legislative influence. Rhode Island Republican Claudine Schneider, perhaps the most liberal House Republican, backed Gingrich. She said, "we were sending a signal [by electing Gingrich]. Basically there is an abuse of power by the Democrats in the House—staff allotment for committees is a joke, for example. Newt will fight for changes."[35] "It's not working for us," complained Olympia Snowe, a leader of women and moderates within the House Republican party. "We need to do something."[36]

"Activists," "outsiders," and "confrontationalists" were more accurate descriptions of Gingrich's key supporters. The common trait of most Gingrich supporters was estrangement from both the Democratic and Republican leadership. These issue-oriented, restless elements in the House GOP arrayed along the entire ideological spectrum, but they joined to form a narrow majority over the accommodating insiders.

Careful media accounts of the Whip race described some of the groups on each side. A fuller explanation is desirable, especially to explain why so many moderate members chose Gingrich. The need for explanation is even greater now that Speaker Gingrich and his allies occupy most of the leadership rungs in the new Republican majority.

This explanatory problem can be largely resolved by addressing some of the weaknesses of analysis that uses roll-call votes. In the modern Congress, floor voting is only one arena where members take their positions. Other arenas include committees, public speeches and letters, caucuses, or other informal groups. The floor is the arena most open to pressure from the party leadership, party colleagues, or interest groups. Consequently, some lawmakers may not vote according to their own views. In recent years the most obvious party leadership sanctions have decreased, but there is more leadership involvement and more pressure to conform. In addition, sanctions from well-financed interest groups have risen as political action committee funding becomes more important in elections. All these pressures distort roll-call vote results.

Other factors may especially distort minority-party voting. The minority party will oppose most initiatives from the majority party. Some minority-party members may regard opposition as the minority party's role, while others may have ideological motivations. The structure of the voting situation may also prompt opposition— procedural unfairness, spending choices either too generous or too meager, resentment over exclusion from the legislative process, allowed amendments too few or too narrow. A vote remains "no," but the motive varies. The House Rules Committee tightened floor procedures during the 1980s and the early 1990s.[37] Tighter procedural controls gave more reasons for more Republicans to vote "no" in protest, a voting outcome that masked other divisions within the GOP. The importance of floor-voting activity may also vary by member of Congress. Some take votes seriously; others may see floor votes as a commodity that can be traded.

Beyond the practical problems of roll-call voting are the philosophical problems—intraparty disagreement about traditional congressional norms, the role of organized party opposition, the value of constructive alternatives, and the substance of relations with the president.

Compounding the difficulty of roll-call analysis is the lessened reliability of traditional measures, such as the Conservative Coalition. Not only have southern Democrats voted more like their party colleagues from across the nation in recent years, but the House Democratic leadership more aggressively pushed floor-vote unity through creative use of leadership innovations. This study will document the extent to which the Democratic Party became more unified at the floor stage, and the tools it employed to promote that unity.

Fortunately a recent explosion in data collection helps develop a new quantitative base for tracing the changes in House Republican factions. Guiding the use of this data are the broader descriptions of House Republicans presented by Connelly and Pitney, Reichley, Rae, and others; and Reiter's dynamic model of intraparty factions.

The first step is to collect data including but moving beyond roll-call voting. This study accomplishes this task in two steps, first by reviewing the new ideological movements affecting the House GOP and, second, by proposing means to identify how adherents of these movements might act. This study divides the available data into three areas: *issue voting, ideological voting patterns,* and *individual associations and behaviors.* Each of these areas has several data elements, which are summarized here, and are explained in greater detail in the appendix.

The *issue-voting* dimension examines voting behavior on economic, social, and foreign policy. The dimension is measured in part by *National Journal (NJ)* scores for each area. In the *National Journal's* scores, members of Congress are rated against their colleagues in each Congress on two zero-to-100 scales, one measuring liberalism and the other measuring conservatism. This analysis uses the liberalism dimension, with zero the most conservative and 100 the most liberal. The issue voting dimension is enhanced by data from the National Taxpayers Union (NTU) for spending issues. The interest group rating complements the *NJ* ratings.

The *ideological patterns* dimension looks at overall voting patterns. It is operationalized by creating a mean *NJ* score from the three issue-based scores. In addition, the ideological dimension uses a relative fiscal conservatism ratio: the ratio of the *NJ* social and foreign policy score average over the *NJ* economic score. This ratio emphasizes the difference between a member's conservatism on economic issues versus noneconomic issues. The higher the ratio, the more liberal the member is on foreign or social policy as compared with economic policy. The purpose is to highlight a pattern of voting that identifies members as especially conservative on economic and budget issues, identifying those members who deviate from the New Deal paradigm that defined liberalism and conservatism in a particular way.

The *individual associations and activity*, or "activity" area, is the most complex. First, it examines individual member interests in the legislative process, broad policy questions, internal influence, or parochial district-based concerns. The primary measure of interest in the legislative process is the "legislative activity score" that compares each member's legislative activity to the mean for House Republicans. This score is also a ratio. The numerator is each member's measurable legislative activity (bills and floor amendments sponsored and cosponsored), and the denominator is the mean legislative activity level of all House Republicans. Additional information fleshes out associations and activities such as each member's stated memberships in informal caucuses, intraparty groups, and congressional committees. The purpose is to stress the associational choices members make across a range of activities. Although the number and identity of committee memberships, for example, are not freely chosen, Fenno[38] and others have linked committee memberships to important aspects of member attitudes. Membership in intraparty groups such as the '92 Group or the Conservative Opportunity Society is almost completely self-selected. Other groups such as the House Wednesday Group and the Republican Study Committee have membership requirements, but the selection criteria of each group channel particular types of members to them. The House Wednesday Group, open by invitation only, used to be clearly identified as a moderate GOP group. Recently, however, it has become broader ideologically and characterized more by legislative creativity and thoughtfulness. Caucus memberships are limited only by individual member choice. The basis for caucus involvement— issue or constituency—is recognized in the literature and is used here to gauge the type of member interest.[39] The activity score also quantifies the total activity level, identifying different levels of activity on national concerns.

The concept behind the activity data is that activity types and levels are measures of norm acceptance in the post-reform House. Members of intraparty committees, such as the '92 Group or the Conservative Opportunity Society, challenged the established GOP party leadership. Members of constituency-oriented bipartisan caucuses preferred bipartisanship and had less interest in partisan concerns. Members with low activity levels indicated lack of attention to Washington issues and, possibly, high acceptance of traditional House norms.

Factions in the 1989 Whip Race

The importance of each dimension appears in a cursory data examination of the two sides in the Gingrich-Madigan race. Aggregated *NJ* economic, social, and foreign policy scores of Gingrich supporters and Madigan supporters are similar, with Gingrich supporters narrowly more conservative.

Additional statistics do not at first appear to shed light on the dynamics of the Whip race. There is some indication that Gingrich's supporters had less service in the House. The average beginning date for House GOP terms was about 1980. For Gingrich supporters, the mean was early 1982, and for Madigan backers it was early 1979.

The new measures, however, provide useful clues about GOP factions. Later chapters scrutinize the data, in the process of describing each House Republican faction. Summary results appear in this context, because they help explain the Gingrich-Madigan Whip race. The factions, and estimated votes in the Gingrich race, are:

Moralists: This group emphasizes moral or value issues. Other distinctive measures are low *NJ* spending and foreign policy scores. They are fast growing, although their members do not usually have long House careers. Moralists numbered about thirty-three in the 101st Congress, and went two to one for Gingrich.

Enterprisers: Enterprisers are conservative, but especially on economic issues in which they focus their activity and interest. They are also busy in all areas of congressional activity, usually the most active of factions. Two-thirds of the thirty-four Enterprisers in the 101st Congress backed Gingrich.

Patricians: These Republicans have moderately liberal voting records across all issues. Patricians are very active, especially in legislation and in national caucuses. Although they are ideologically to the left of Gingrich, they became increasingly frustrated by growing Democratic roadblocks to GOP participation in the legislative process. The eleven Patricians in the 101st Congress were predominately from the East and had long tenure on the Hill. In the March 1989 Whip race, they split seven to four for Madigan.

Moderates: Thirty-three Republicans with moderate voting scores across issues, averaging about 35 on each *NJ* issue dimension, could be identified as Moderates in the 101st Congress. They are very active in the legislative process, and are found mostly in the Great Lakes and Mid-Atlantic, especially New Jersey and New York. Eastern Moderates were slightly for Gingrich, Midwesterners for Madigan.

Stalwarts: These are the most traditional Republicans, and numbered in the mid-forties in the most recent Congresses. They are uniformly conservative in voting, and fairly partisan in their outlook. Stalwarts sided slightly with Madigan, with differences based on region and the extent of conservatism, as more moderate Midwesterners went with Madigan and more conservative Stalwarts from other regions supported Gingrich.

Provincials: These Republicans are conservative, but they vote much more liberally on spending than on international or social issues since their main concern is servicing the interest of their poor, rural districts. They are highly pragmatic and, while the GOP was a House minority, depended upon personal relationships with Democrats to obtain benefits for their districts. The eighteen Provincials voted two to one for Madigan.

Placeholders: This faction is moderate in overall voting, but votes more conservatively on economics than on social or foreign policy. Some have strong libertarian tendencies, while others recall the isolationism of Taft Republicans. They are long-standing GOP members, and are uncomfortable with the new activism and ideology of the GOP. The more than one dozen Placeholders voted almost unanimously for Madigan.

Simple ideology does not fully explain these divisions, although ideology is important.[40] But the new information in this analysis is more important. Legislative activity is critical—the number, type and relative importance of caucus, standing committee, party committee, and intraparty group attachments. Those interested in national themes and estranged from the previous leadership tended to back Gingrich, and the proportion of activist groups supporting the Georgian grew as group ideology became more conservative. Madigan's support went the other way—his support was strongest with the most passive and moderate groups, with passivity explaining his support more than ideology.

The two groups most influenced by issues and most opposed to congressional norms—Enterprisers and Moralists—were critical to Gingrich's coalition. Policy-oriented Moderates and Patricians were cross-pressured, drawn to Gingrich by his emphasis on issues but generally voting more in line with Madigan. These groups split almost evenly, with the younger and more aggressive moderates in the '92 Group supporting Gingrich most strongly. Those least interested in new issues and most comfortable with traditional norms formed the bulk of Madigan's support.

Reinforcement of Factional Divisions

The divisions in the 1989 Whip race were further revealed in the organization of the Republican Conference in the 103rd Congress after the 1992 elections. The takeover of the party by aggressive conservatives was ratified in the new majority leadership and organizational decisions made by the new majority two years later, after the successful 1994 elections.

Several leadership slots were contested at the beginning of the 103rd Congress, some of them open seats and others with incumbents. In every case, more traditional and moderate candidates lost to more activist conservatives.[41] In an open seat race for conference secretary, Texan Tom DeLay overwhelmed Bill Gradison; and Nancy Johnson of Connecticut lost her challenge to incumbent conference vice-chair, Bill McCollum of Florida.[42]

The key race, however, was for chair of the Republican Conference, the number-three leadership post in the party. Incumbent Jerry Lewis of California lost by a narrow 88–84 margin to Dick Armey of Texas.[43] Armey's challenge hinged on the charge that Lewis was too cozy with the Democratic majority. Lewis had used his position as ranking minority member on the Legislative Branch Appropriations subcommittee to broker institution-building deals and blunt attacks on the operations of Congress. In many ways, the 1992 Armey-Lewis conference race mirrored the dynamics of the 1989 Gingrich-Madigan Whip race, although many of the strategic details of the campaign differed, and more than one-third of the Republican conference had entered the House after 1989. Although Lewis was criticized by some younger GOP members for not being confrontational enough, Armey did not directly campaign on a pledge of greater partisan conflict. Armey based most of his campaign, rather, on two messages—a return to economics-based policy, and an appeal to change particularly targeted at younger members. Armey asserted that his PhD in economics and his ranking position on the Joint Economic Committee could help the party develop a more appealing domestic policy message, and that he would ensure the participation of all members, especially junior members, in conference activities.[44] Most interpreters of the race saw it as a showdown between the more ideological conservatives, generally favoring Armey, and the more traditional and pragmatic wing in which Lewis had risen.[45]

The race was for the most part run honorably, with Armey focusing on incumbent conservative activists and incoming freshmen. Armey had support from Gingrich and like-minded members, but he ran for the position largely on his own. Lewis's strategy was less clear. After Armey announced his challenge Lewis apparently helped kill a huge federal project in Texas—the superconducting supercollider—a move that consolidated Texans against him. Lewis also opposed an Armey school choice amendment, reportedly more out of personal animosity than policy disagreement.[46]

While it is rare for an incumbent party leader to fall in the absence of personal scandal or electoral disaster, Lewis fell to Armey. The freshman class of 1992 apparently was decisive, as an estimated thirty-five to forty newcomers in a class of forty-seven supported the challenger. These freshmen interpreted the Armey victory as a victory for activism, not necessarily conservatism. John Linder of Georgia said the freshman class was "looking for activity."[47] "People are quick to pin a conservative label on us," said newcomer Deborah Pryce of Ohio. "I prefer the label activist."[48]

Armey interpreted his victory as endorsing his calls for a return to economic issues as the basis for unity, to cultivate talent in the younger members, and to establish a brainier attack on Democratic programs. "What we want to do is discover who our geniuses are and back them,"[49] Armey said. The themes articulated by Armey in 1992 in many ways echoed Gingrich's 1989 promises to create a more responsible party with a more positive agenda.

With both in the leadership, these plans could finally be developed. The 1994 House campaign strategy was the first concrete outcome of the Gingrich-Armey plan to promote a positive Republican agenda targeted directly to voters. Their "Contract With America," envisioned by Gingrich, defined by Armey, and influenced by activists across most of the party's ideological spectrum, was the first product of a newly aggressive House GOP.

The contract stuck to economic and reformist themes, and was presented with populist and progressive arguments. In addition, it avoided most conservative social agenda items such as abortion, school prayer, and minority rights that divide the party and the targeted electorate of "Reagan Democrats" and 1992 Perot voters.

While its success was not universal, the contract helped to make the 1994 off-year elections more focused on issues, and on those issues in which Republicans have advantages. Old Democratic appeals had less legitimacy and in some cases were seen as attempts to run from the Democratic party. The lessened impact of individualistic appeals usually made by Democrats was a critical difference in many elections. And while the House GOP landslide may not have been a mandate for the specific provisions of the contract, it seemed to be a clear endorsement of the strategy of creating a responsible House Republican Conference with a focused legislative agenda.

The 1994 organizational conference ratified the agenda of the now-dominant activist conservative House GOP leadership. The elements of the contract were reaffirmed as the GOP's prime objectives. The conference also limited the terms of the Speaker and committee leaders, centralized control of committee selection and floor scheduling at the top party leadership level, defunded legislative service organizations, and reorganized the internal operation of the House and its support offices.

The Changed Face of House Republicans

The remainder of this book begins by exploring the environment in which House Republican factions emerged in the post-reform era. Chapter two looks at the internal influences on the creation of House Republican factions. These influences, most of which have made factions harder to identify by customary measures, include the movement of agenda control in the Democratic House from committee leaders to party leaders, and the increasing entrepreneurial activity of members.

External influences, which have served mostly to increase the number of factions, are discussed in chapter three. The major external influence on the GOP is the wave of conservative ideological movements that were increasingly active beginning in the mid-1970s. Internal and external influences combined to create a more complex set of factions in the House Republican party.

The four more activist factions are discussed in chapter four, with special focus on the emerging dominant realigning coalition of Enterprisers and Moralists. Chapter five examines the three factions less active in the Washington policy arena—the Stalwarts, Provincials, and Placeholders.

The concluding chapter six evaluates the House Republican party in its new status as the congressional majority. It looks at which factions in the party have become ascendant, examines their power in the strategy and outcome of the 1994 elections, and explores the implications of the election results on the House of Representatives and the new congressional majority party.

Notes

1. Warren Brooks, "Georgia Gnat with a Whip?" *Washington Times*, 17 March 1989, F1, 4.

2. Janet Hook, "Battle for Whip Pits Partisans Against Party Pragmatists," *Congressional Quarterly Weekly Report* 47 (18 March 1989): 563–65.

3. John P. Gregg, "After Dick Cheney's Departure: Now Who'll Lead House GOP?" *Roll Call*, 13 March 1989, 1.

4. Don Phillips, "Reps. Madigan, Gingrich Vie for GOP Post," *Washington Post,* 16 March 1989, A6.

5. For studies of recent minority party leadership races see Robert L. Peabody, "The Ford-Halleck Minority Leadership Contest, 1965," in *Leadership in Congress* (Boston: Little, Brown, 1976); and Charles O. Jones, *The Minority Party in Congress* (Boston: Little, Brown, 1970).

6. Robin Toner, "GOP Focuses on Cheney Succession," *New York Times*, 14 March 1989, B7.

7. Garrison Nelson, "Partisan Patterns of House Leadership Change, 1789–1977," *American Political Science Review* 71 (1977): 918–39; and Maureen Roberts Romans, "Republican Leadership Fights on the House of Representatives: The Causes of Conflict, 1895–1931," paper presented at the 1977

Annual Meeting of the American Political Science Association, Washington, D.C., 1–4 September 1977.

8. Toner, B7.

9. Hook, "Battle For Whip," 565.

10. Hook, "Battle For Whip," 565.

11. John P. Gregg, "Gingrich, Madigan In Whip Showdown," *Roll Call*, 20 March 1989, 23.

12. Richard E. Cohen, "Gingrich: From Gadfly to Whip," *National Journal* 21 (25 March 1989): 743.

13. Brooks, F4.

14. Gloria Borger, "Dennis the Menace Comes in From the Cold," *U.S. News and World Report*, 27 March 1989, 25.

15. Janet Hook, "Gingrich's Selection as Whip Reflects GOP Discontent," *Congressional Quarterly Weekly Report* 47 (25 March 1989): 626.

16. Robin Toner, "Race for Whip: Hyperspeed vs. Slow Motion," *New York Times*, 22 March 1989, A22.

17. Paul A. Gigot, "Neutron Newt Could Become GOP's Coelho," *Wall Street Journal*, 17 March 1989, 18.

18. Wesley Pruden, "Building a Fire Under the GOP," *Washington Times*, 22 March 1989, A4.

19. Pruden, A4.

20. *Toward A More Responsible Two-Party System* (New York: Rinehart & Co., 1950), first appearing as a supplement to *The American Political Science Review* 44 (September 1950).

21. James MacGregor Burns, *The Deadlock of Democracy* (Englewood Cliffs, N.J.: Prentice-Hall, 1963, Spectrum Books, 1967), passim.

22. See, for example, James L. Sundquist, "Needed: A Political Theory for the New Era of Coalition Government," *Political Science Quarterly* 103 (Winter 1988): 613–35 passim, for a definition of the problem; Gary W. Cox and Samuel Kernell, eds., *The Politics of Divided Government* (Boulder, Colo.: Westview Press, 1991) for a review of the most important issues; and Byron E. Shafer, "The Notion of an Electoral Order: The Structure of Electoral Politics at the Accession of George Bush," unpublished manuscript (Oxford University, Cambridge, 1990), passim, for an attempt to move beyond the realignment-dealignment-rolling realignment debate.

23. For a recent sympathetic exposition see, for example, Michael Malbin, "Factions and Incentives in Congress," *Public Interest* 86 (Winter 1987): 91–108.

24. Fred Barnes, "Newtered," *New Republic*, 24 April 1989, 9.

25. Michael Kranish, "U.S. House Faces Big Decisions on Leadership," *Boston Globe*, 21 March 1989, 8.

26. Norman J. Ornstein, "Gingrich Spells Trouble for Bush," *New York Times*, 27 March 1989, A17.

27. Richard E. Cohen, "Gingrich: Don't Expect 'Kinder, Gentler' Politics," *Los Angeles Times*, 2 April 1989, V3.

28. In most prior research, the term "faction" has been used to describe intraparty divisions ranging from cohesive and fully organized blocs to temporary, shifting, and personality-oriented groups, and to all variations between (Howard Reiter, "Intra-Party Cleavages in the United States Today," *Western Political Quarterly* 34 [1981]: 287). This analysis states that a faction exists when there is a group of legislators holding a set of voting and behavior patterns that together define a particular perspective on various issues, roles, duties, and opportunities facing legislators. Under such a definition, a congressional faction may not be formally organized or institutionalized, although many in the GOP are. The activity patterns of a faction, however, must be relatively stable over time, and its members must regularly repeat observed patterns.

29. Don Phillips and Tom Kenworthy, "Gingrich Elected House GOP Whip," *Washington Post*, 23 March 1989, A10.

30. Phillips and Kenworthy, 1.

31. The author has a list of expected votes of each House Republican for either candidate, obtained from a vote counter for one of the candidates. The vote count fits exactly with the vote totals on each side and with all known public positions stated before or after the vote. The count could have double errors; however, that is unlikely given the extensive verification efforts.

32. Donald Lambro, "Vote for Gingrich Was Vote Against Michel," *Washington Times*, 23 March 1989, A4.

33. See, for example, Hook, "Battle," 563.

34. Cohen, "Gadfly to Whip," 743.

35. Myra MacPherson, "Newt Gingrich: Point Man in a House Divided," *Washington Post*, 12 June 1989, C9.

36. Borger, 25.

37. See, for example, Stanley Bach and Steven S. Smith, *Managing Uncertainty in the House of Representatives* (Washington, D.C.: Brookings Institution, 1988), and later claims by the House Republican leadership over "closed rules" and other provisions designed to ensure floor outcomes favorable to the House majority party.

38. Richard Fenno, *Congressmen in Committees* (Boston: Little, Brown, 1973).

39. See, for example, Susan Webb Hammond, Daniel Mulhollan and Arthur G. Stevens, Jr., "Informal Congressional Caucuses and Agenda Setting," *Western Political Quarterly* 38 (1985): 583–605, in which party, national issue, regional, state, district, and other bases for caucus membership are identified.

40. The first two faction names were inspired by Times Mirror, Inc. *The People, Press, & Politics: A Times Mirror Study of the American Electorate Conducted By The Gallup Organization* (Los Angeles: Times Mirror, Inc., September 1987); Stalwarts and Moderates by Reichley; the others were the author's own inspiration.

41. Phil Kuntz, "GOP Moderates Take a Hit In Caucus Elections," *Congressional Quarterly Weekly Report* 50 (12 December 1992): 3781.

42. Kuntz, 3781.

43. Richard E. Cohen, "Capitol Hill Update," *National Journal* (12 December 1992): 2844.

44. Cohen, "Update," 21.

45. "Armey Will Run For Lewis' Post," *Congressional Quarterly Weekly Report* 50 (6 June 1992): 1587.

46. Timothy J. Burger, " 'Far Right' Wins GOP Leadership Positions," *Roll Call*, 10 December 1992, 12.

47. Beth Donovan, "Freshmen Throw Weight Around, Make Their Parties Listen," *Congressional Quarterly Weekly Report* 50 (12 December 1992): 3794.

48. Donovan, 3794.

49. Allen Freedman, "An 'Uppity Minority Guy' Takes Charge," *National Journal* 25 (16 January 1993): 148.

Chapter 2

The Partisan Aspects of Congressional Change

Congress scholars call the late 1960s through the middle 1970s a time of "reform," and identify the time from the late 1970s to the middle 1990s as the "post-reform era." The wave of changes with the Republican takeover has not yet gained a label. The reform era saw greater rank-and-file access to power, while the post-reform era brought a steady trend toward centralization of power within the majority-party leadership, rather than committees.

A traditional organizing principle of research on Congress has been its norms.[1] In the post-reform era Republicans came to see norms as partisan tools to aid, cover, and justify expanded Democratic power. The four traditional norms in the House of Representatives are seniority, specialization, reciprocity, and institutional loyalty.[2] The seniority norm is apparent when committee chairs and party leadership positions go to senior members. This norm would be violated when, for example, younger members conspicuously supported a leadership candidate not blessed by the sitting leaders, as occurred in the 1989 GOP Whip race. The specialization norm requires members to focus on their committees' jurisdictions and stay out of other areas. Violations occur when members join ideological caucuses, or organize intraparty groups that address a broad range of issues. Clearly, Gingrich's Conservative Opportunity Society violated this norm. The reciprocity norm involves matters of personal conduct—horse-trading, log-rolling, and mutual comity should govern personal relationships. Gingrich probably was most noted for violating this norm. The institutional loyalty norm contends that no issue is important enough to destroy the chamber. House Democratic Whip Tony Coelho often said

31

that Gingrich wanted to "destroy" the institution, but the Georgian's activities cannot fairly be seen as targeted against the House.[3] His activities are more appropriately characterized as violations of specialization and reciprocity, not of institutional loyalty. For example, in the spring of 1984 Gingrich and his fellow activist Robert Walker of Pennsylvania took to the House floor to publicize a Republican staff report charging several Democrats of having a "radical worldview" that led them to look first to American policy, rather than to communism or to the Soviet Union, as the source for many international problems. These floor speeches led to the famous "camscam" incident in which Speaker Thomas P. O'Neill ordered House cameras to pan the chamber to show that no one was listening to similar charges Walker was making the next day. O'Neill's unprecedented partisan use of the cameras and his later floor speech against these tactics that included such vitriol that it was ruled out of order, both made Gingrich a star and served to illustrate the difficulty Democrats were having in distinguishing between fair criticism of individual members of their party and unfair attacks on the institution.[4]

Norms are created and sustained largely by the majority party. The minority party may not agree with these norms but it is usually forced to accept them. The longer a party remains in the majority and the more partisan that majority becomes, however, the more the minority party will identify norms with the majority party's hegemony instead of the institution's integrity.

Minority-party members obey or break these norms, but they cannot change them. House institutions opened up in the reform era, diminishing seniority and specialization and increasing the need for reciprocity and institutional loyalty while at the same time creating an open climate in which they were likely to flourish. In the post-reform era, House operations began to close again around party leaders, partly reversing the reform era's effects. While the need for reciprocity and institutional loyalty was still high, the environment did not encourage their maintenance. The key partisan impact of the post-reform era was to increase party tensions.

Institutional Changes: Committees, Leadership, and Floor

Post-reform changes have affected House Republicans and Democrats in different ways. The reform era created more opportunities for entrepreneurs in both parties. But by the late 1970s, more aggressive majority leadership and greater restrictions on debate diminished the opportunity for minority party members to participate in legislative work. Over time, these diminished legislative opportunities turned more House Republicans against the norms of Congress, making even moderate Republicans more hostile toward Democrats' control of the institution and more united on traditional measures of party unity. By the later years of the post-reform era, even the most stalwart of members were concluding the House was unfair, with Bob Michel declaring in 1990 that "the Majority has turned this House into a den of inequity."[5]

Few scholars have noted these changes. If they have, they have blamed the Reagan administration's confrontational stance toward Congress. But the trends toward consolidation and partisanship began before 1981. While Reagan's confrontational style may have encouraged a congressional response, at most it accelerated an established trend.

Committees

Most committee-related indicators show a pattern of expansion and democratization that ended before 1980. The number of House committees increased steadily from the mid-1950s through the mid-1970s, with 130 panels in the 84th Congress of 1955–56 and a record 204 such groups twenty years later. Most of the growth here was in standing committees, not in special, joint and *ad hoc* committees. During the committee expansion phase, the opportunities for "committee government" and "subcommittee government" grew apace.

But the trend changed. For example, between 1976 and 1992 Democrats allowed an approximate 10 percent drop in standing committee and subcommittee numbers. There were eighty-three of these panels in 1955, 151 in the 94th Congress of 1975–76, and 135 in 1992.[6]

Select or special committees, on the other hand, grew consistently, exhibiting the largest proportional growth in the post-reform era. There were seven select and special committee units in 1955 and seventeen in 1990, before they were abolished in early 1993 in anticipation of later reforms.[7] Select committees had no lawmaking powers. They flourished, however, because the issues reflected in their names—Hunger, Aging, Youth and Families, and Narcotics Abuse and Control—had public appeal.

The growth of select committees, together with the decline of standing subcommittees, suggests that the committee system accommodated more entrepreneurial members by allowing greater expression of ideas rather than allowing more hands in the congressional pork barrel.

Committee staff numbers also changed dramatically. House committee staffs increased twelvefold between 1947 and 1987, with the greatest growth in the 1970s. These staffs grew almost threefold in the 1970s, from 729 in 1970 to more than 1,900 by 1980. This staff growth did not repeat in the 1980s. In 1990, for example, House committee staff numbered almost exactly 2,000, only 6 percent higher than in 1979.[8]

The number of standing committees and staff size began to change in the late 1970s, *before* the Reagan administration and immediately after the sixteen-seat House Democratic losses in the 1978 elections. This timing suggests that the reduced number of substantive panels was related either to the Democrats' need to organize policy differently or to a new policy environment emerging in the late 1970s. The timing also suggests that the reduction in standing subcommittees was not a congressional response to an aggressive president of the opposition party.

The increase in select committees and the symbolic representation they afford is also important. Growth of these committees may have stemmed from different interests of new members of Congress, the relative scarcity of discretionary spending, or a combination of these and other factors. In any case, the primary advantage of dispersed standing committee authority—to advance legislation creating or expanding federal programs—diminished in the late 1970s, before Reagan. Limiting slots on standing legislative subcommittees could not be accomplished in isolation. Members' individual resources were growing and needed to be accommodated. One accommodation was to expand the select committees.

Histories of congressional committee changes over the last few decades are portrayed as a movement from oligarchy in the 1960s to dispersion in the 1970s to chaos and deadlock in the 1980s, with most research on congressional committees dating the end of standing committee growth too late.[9] Richard Fenno,[10] writing in 1965, already found a congressional committee system moving toward decentralization. The 1960s House that Fenno observed was essentially a semi-oligarchical body held together by two clusters of norms—one supporting the leadership system of each party and the other supporting good working relations between each set of leaders. Interparty conflict was diminished by trust, friendship, and consultation at the top.[11]

Fenno used the word "oligarchy" to describe the mid-1960s House; ten years later Harvey Mansfield worried about a dispersion of authority.[12] Fenno's Congress held the potential for collective strength. Mansfield doubted that members empowered by subcommittee autonomy could subordinate their freedom to collective force. He found that increases in salary, staff, work space, logistical support, and subsidized conveniences contributed to individualism and professionalism.

Mansfield believed that these changes hampered majority building, but that was not the most important outcome. The critical effect was, rather, to make room for a wider range of personality types. The author labeled these new types as "miners, sappers, missionaries, entrepreneurs, brokers, broken-field runners and players to the grandstand."[13] Each type intended to make a mark in Congress, but the marks differed. Mansfield suggested that there are legitimate representational functions beyond lawmaking. He also suggested that Congress kindles diverse individual ambitions, and individual members can use the array of resources at their disposal to advance these ambitions.

Mansfield observed, almost as a footnote, that then-new reforms of the early 1970s (for example, the 1974 budget changes and the growing power of the Democratic caucus) were attempts to encourage cross-committee consensus among representatives who had larger committee and individual resource bases.[14] He did not elaborate on his point that compensatory leadership attempts to centralize power were starting, even as committee dispersion and individual entrepreneurialism were just beginning to be noted in the literature.

For many years, most congressional research overlooked Mansfield's point. One possible explanation for this oversight is related to a false assumption about the congressional norms of apprenticeship, reciprocity, specialization, and muted partisanship. Most scholars assume that these norms are permanent and independent of external influences. But norms may not only be partisan; they also may depend upon external variables. In this case, the important external changes were economic—the end of escalating real federal revenues from higher inflation and worsening economic performance.

The legislative implications of the lean fiscal years that began in the mid-1970s may not have been fully understood at first. Scholars may have missed how distributionist lawmaking hinged on steady economic growth. With fewer real tax dollars to spend, Congress had less need for the newly created subcommittee specialization. Worsening economic conditions meant that instead of a broad agenda full of new and potential programs, the House faced a constricted agenda of cutting back.

In terms of placing the responsibility for heightened House partisanship on Reagan or on the late-1970s economy, it seems more fitting to examine the fiscal austerity that began during the Carter administration. In response, the House moved to a narrow "four-bill" system based on money—a budget resolution, a continuing appropriations bill, a supplemental appropriations bill, and a reconciliation package of spending cuts. This new agenda was built upon the politics of fiscal scarcity and all other legislation was of secondary importance. Members who influenced the four major bills were the important players; others played only on the fringes.

Log-rolling and mutual accommodation, the customary behavior under congressional norms, depend on a growing economy and on significant amounts of cross-party cooperation. Assuming that these norms are nonpartisan and permanent makes individualists—either ideological agitators or local ombudsmen—seem less legitimate.

Misidentifying the point at which dispersion of House power began to reverse results in a mistaken classification of its causes. For example, a common explanation for partisan reconsolidation has been Reagan's aggressive antigovernment agenda. Consolidation thus becomes justified as a logical response to Republican partisanship instead of, more likely, the Democratic leadership's unilateral decision to consolidate power in party organs. An unfortunate consequence is to excuse the majority party for excluding the minority party.

By the late 1980s, research finally began to note that congressional decentralization had ended. In many cases, too, the appropriate causes were being identified. In the 1980s a few "supercommittees" had wrestled power from the many subcommittees created the decade before. Decision making on most key issues was controlled by a few committee leaders under party leadership prodding.

There are also partisan and policy consequences to the end of subcommittee growth. In the early 1970s and before, the two parties and their leaders comfortably displayed traditional log-rolling behaviors for the benefit of enough individual Republicans at least to continue the appearance of bipartisanship. This informal bipartisan accommodation muted partisanship because it allowed significant participation by minority party members. Beginning in the late 1970s, however, legislative power began to reconcentrate in Democratic committee and party heads.

The problem facing Democratic party heads in a tight economic and fiscal environment with a dispersed congressional committee system was new. The problem no longer was how to achieve a majority that included members of both parties, but rather how to achieve enough Democratic unity so that Republicans were not needed. Six House committees—Ways and Means, Appropriation, Energy and Commerce, Budget, Armed Services, and Rules—controlled nearly all important legislation.[15] Most bargaining took place among committee or subcommittee chairs and the Democratic party leadership. The Republican influence in the stunning fiscal victories of President Reagan in 1981, and to a lesser extent in 1982, were flukes, even though the fiscal consequences of the events lasted longer.

Because budget legislation dominates Congress, the minority party in the post-reform era was effectively shut out of its legislative role since the early 1980s. The pressure of fiscal scarcity shifted the locus of power away from subcommittee and other substantive leaders to political and partisan leaders. Bipartisanship became less frequent, both because it was more difficult and because the catalyst for coalition building came from party leaders.

Party-led coalition building is fostered by limiting standing committee and subcommittee numbers. Consequently, the major partisan implication of subcommittee retrenchment is that Republicans were less needed by Democrats to forge coalitions. Increasingly overlooked by their majority party peers, senior Republicans became more sympathetic to GOP partisan appeals.

Leadership

Most scholars looked at the 1970s reforms and declared that power in Congress was now open to even the most junior members. They forgot about Republicans, who now had *less* access to power. These new limits on minority participation had chiefly been accomplished by augmenting the power of the Speaker.

The Speaker's renewed power was most evident in control over the Rules Committee, task forces, and the Steering and Policy Committee. In 1975 House Democrats greatly strengthened the Speaker by authorizing him to appoint the Democratic members of the Rules Committee and to name the members of a Steering and Policy Committee to make committee assignments for Democrats. In the view of at least one scholar, 1975 marked the highest point of majority leadership power since 1910.[16]

The partisan tensions of the 1980s further expanded the Democrats' "openness" to one another, and decreased Democratic openness to Republicans. The result was greater party unity scores for both parties, and a weakened "conservative coalition" of Republicans and southern Democrats. Party unity scores began rising in the late 1970s, especially among House Democrats. By 1983, Democratic party unity topped that of Republicans, and for the twelve years from 1982 through 1993, Democratic party unity averaged 85 percent, nearly ten points higher than party unity among Republicans.[17] By the 103rd Congress of 1993–94, northern and southern Democrats had become similar enough to push the "conservative coalition" success rate to its lowest level ever recorded.[18]

This path toward a more partisan House reflected leadership innovations in the post-reform era. The innovations are well chronicled even as their partisan implications are usually overlooked. Barbara Sinclair was one of the first to note attempts by the majority leadership to cope with a decentralized House by "involving as many House Democrats as possible in the coalition building process" before legislation would come to the floor.[19] She pointed out that the 1970s reforms had increased the number of "significant actors" within the Democratic caucus needed to form "winning coalitions." She also pointed out that the personalities and reelection needs of younger Democrats (such as those elected in the 1974 Watergate landslide) required that they be accommodated in developing legislation. These institutional changes and individual needs would by themselves lead to a higher level of "unpredictability" in House floor voting outcomes, unless there was more party control of policy content and floor procedures to counter these trends.[20]

In a separate 1981 article Sinclair explored the new phenomenon of the Speaker's task force.[21] She noted that the Speaker's task forces helped Democratic party leaders perform "both of their primary functions—building winning coalitions and 'keeping peace in the family.' "[22] She found that a combination of rules changes, membership turnover, norm changes, and new issues had created a "less predictable" House environment. Sinclair identified mischievous Republican amendments as egregious examples of this unwanted and unjustified unpredictability.[23] Speaker task forces justly restored predictability by unifying the party around legislative alternatives and floor strategies long before voting was scheduled. Unity increased because task forces socialized Democrats by including junior members and diverse party elements. Task force efforts were "successful" because all legislative initiatives shepherded by task forces passed the

House and did so without "crippling" floor amendments.[24] No negative implications of the task force innovation, such as the reduced substantive role of the minority party in the legislative process and the lost political benefits of bipartisan action, were mentioned.

By 1984, innovative Democratic leadership tactics were more concrete and their partisan implications were becoming obvious. Burdett Loomis focused on formal leadership slots and found that one outcome of the Democrats' interest in intraparty unity was "increasing partisanship" on the House floor.[25] He discovered that there were partisan implications of the Speaker's new power to choose members to the Rules Committee and the Steering and Policy Committee.[26] He also noted that the number of formal leadership positions expanded from sixty-four in the early 1970s to, depending on the definition used, either eighty-seven or 103 in the early 1980s.[27] These new leadership positions were concentrated in the Whip system and in other areas related to building a unified Democratic position on floor amendments and procedures before bills reached the floor.[28]

Partisanship encouraged by the majority leadership increased over the decade of the 1980s. A House veteran with ties to Republicans noted in 1989 that "to an extent not imagined only 15 years ago, and even significantly advanced just since 1985, the elected leaders of the House of Representatives have assumed substantial new responsibilities at the expense of committee chairs and other senior figures."[29] This author chronicled the development of complex rules and other floor procedures, noting that they had been employed to the advantage of the Democratic party leadership.

In 1994 Sinclair published the results of a longitudinal study of Democratic leadership involvement in issues from 1969 to the early 1990s, providing hard evidence of increased House partisanship.[30] In the 91st Congress (1969–71), the House Democratic leadership was involved in less than half of the items on the congressional agenda, and on only one-quarter was that involvement major. By 1990, however, Sinclair found that the Democratic leadership was involved in nearly three-fourths of all agenda items and tried to control directly the outcome of more than half the bills the House considered.[31]

Another area where partisan control of the legislative agenda appeared was the practice of bill referral. Majority-party leaders helped build intraparty majorities through developing substitutes for the several versions of "multiple-referral" bills that committees have approved. The multiple-referral bills, when reported by various committees, often appeared in several different versions, since different

Chapter 2

TABLE 2.1
Multiple Referral Bills in the House
(Percentage of All Bills Referred)

				Congress				
95th	96th	97th	98th	99th	100th	101st	102nd	103rd
Percentage of Bills 10.3	11.7	9.6	11.6	14.0	17.5	18.2	18.2	20.3

Source: Davidson and Oleszek, *Congress and Its Members*, 4th ed. (Washington, D.C.: Congressional Quarterly Press, 1994), 224.

committees conducted different sets of hearings and mark-ups. The several competing versions of the same bill enabled majority-party leaders to forge a "compromise" bill, usually behind closed doors in meetings among only party members. As table 2.1 shows, multiple referral bills grew significantly throughout the post-reform era.

The percentage of bills subject to multiple referral rose in every congress except for one, the 97th Congress of 1981–82, the first congress of Ronald Reagan's first term, and the point in the post-reform era at which Republican House strength was the highest. The growing number of multiple-referral bills is, thus, another measure of the growing partisanship of the House. As Bach and Smith note, "the development of these substitutes frequently excludes committee Republicans and can reverse victories the minority won during committee markup."[32]

This increased involvement of party leaders in agenda control affected both parties. For Democrats, it led to greater loyalty among rank-and-file members as party leaders became more involved in urging members to support more liberal party positions. It also made legislative outcomes more representative of the dominant liberal wing of the party, from which most of the leadership originated. For Republicans, however, the increased partisanship further alienated them from the legislative process.

"Leadership innovations" such as the Speaker's task force were efforts to accommodate diversity within the majority party; they were not intended to resolve differences between the parties. Majority leadership consolidation efforts severely diminished minority opportunities to participate in legislative work, decreasing the representative nature of the House as the post-reform era continued.

Floor

Data on House floor activity reinforce the story of greater Democratic partisanship and control between 1980 and 1994. There were fewer bills being introduced, fewer amendments offered, and fewer bills passed; and those that did pass were controlled by the Democratic leadership. The number of bills introduced in Congress peaked in the 95th Congress of 1977–78 at more than 15,500. By the 102nd Congress, members had authored only a combined total of 7,700 bills.[33] Floor voting also hinted at rising limitations. Recorded votes peaked in 1978 at 834 and fell to the mid-400s by 1991.[34] The number of House floor amendments offered to appropriations bills averaged more than 150 from 1978 through 1980; by 1982 only fifty-nine total amendments were offered to the thirteen annual regular spending bills.[35]

The complexity of floor rules is a key gauge of partisanship. Bach and Smith noted that in the early post-reform 95th Congress of 1977–78, 83 percent of single-committee measures (bills referred to only one committee before being reported to the floor) and 75 percent of all bills had open rules. Only 8.4 percent of single committee bills and 13.5 percent of all bills had either "restrictive" or "complex" rules when debated on the floor.[36] By the 99th Congress of 1985–86, in contrast, only 55 percent of single-committee bills, and less than half of all bills, had open rules. More than 30 percent of single-committee bills and 36.6 percent of all legislation were considered under restricted rules.[37] In the 103rd Congress of 1993–94, just over 20 percent of all bills debated on the House floor had open rules, whereas nearly 80 percent of bills were debated under some type of restriction.[38]

Statistics on rules involving key issues are even more striking. In the 95th Congress of 1977–78, 70.6 percent of "key" bills had open rules. Eight years later only 13.6 percent of "key" bills were open to

TABLE 2.2
Percentage of Restrictive Floor Rules
(95th through 103rd Congresses)

	Congress								
	95th	**96th**	**97th**	**98th**	**99th**	**100th**	**101st**	**102nd**	**103rd**
Percentage Of Rules	15	25	25	32	43	46	55	66	79

Sources: Rules Committee Calendars and *Surveys of Activities, 95th–102nd Congresses*, and "Notices of Action Taken," Committee on Rules, 103rd Congress.

unlimited amendment.[39] The percentage of these measures subject to amendment fell from 25 percent in the 94th Congress of 1975–1976 to only 14 percent in the 99th Congress, and lower in later Congresses.[40] These data further confirm that it became more difficult for minorities to express differences with majority positions on the House floor. Floor debate was limited, and the outcomes were controlled.

Some important implications of floor changes are not captured by statistics. The House Rules Committee fashions House floor voting guidelines. After 1975, the majority-party leadership had new power over the Rules Committee and it was only a matter of time before this power was exercised to greater partisan advantage. That partisanship maximized between 1980 and 1994. In 1981, Speaker O'Neill had promised Republicans that there would be a clean vote on spending reductions proposed by President Reagan. But instead of allowing for the single vote Republicans wanted, O'Neill directed the Rules Committee to divide the cuts into six separate packages, and to strip all GOP provisions that added additional spending in certain areas to ease the pain of cuts. To support Reagan, representatives would have to cast more than a half-dozen votes, most of them against highly popular programs without any provisions offering offsetting benefits. While the Democratic leadership ploy narrowly failed as some House Democrats voted with Republicans against the rule, it sowed the seeds of GOP distrust of structured floor rules. In the later years under Speaker O'Neill, House Democratic leaders more and more frequently told the Rules Committee to craft special rules to limit amendments and structure floor debate to increase the probability of outcomes favorable to House Democratic leaders. The Democratic leadership thereby gained influence in defining the House's menu of alternatives; the Republican leadership could only bargain with the menu or protest its limits.[41]

When Jim Wright became Speaker in 1987, he strengthened leadership power over the Rules Committee. He immediately began to intervene to decide the terms of special floor rules for major legislation. His most infamous moments of procedural authoritarianism were in October 1987 and March 1988. In 1987 in a dispute over a reconciliation bill, the House defeated a Wright-written rule to consider welfare reform together with the spending-cut bill. The rule failed, and rather than let the matter rest for a day as normal procedures require, Wright adjourned the House and immediately reconvened it, creating a second legislative day in which a new rule could be considered. On a later vote on the same matter, Wright delayed closing the voting time until he could convince a freshman Democrat, Jim Chapman, to switch his vote to the party position and ensure a Democratic victory. The 1988 controversy was over military aid to the *contras*. Wright had apparently promised Republican Leader Michel a clean vote on a Republican aid package, but later directed the Rules Committee to write a rule for floor debate that buried the Republican alternative. Albeit expansive, Wright's exercise of authority at these and many other times was the logical conclusion of a longer-term trend of making rules the tools of Democratic leaders.[42]

Nowhere is this seen more clearly than in the growing partisanship of votes on House floor rules. Voting divisions on rules have moved from consensual to highly partisan in the post-reform era, as table 2.3 shows.

The third and fourth columns of the table are two measures of party conflict over rules. Together they provide a clear picture of the growing partisanship of rules. The third column lists the total percentage of consensual votes on floor rules, defined as 90 percent of both parties supporting the rule. While about half of all rules were consensual in

TABLE 2.3
Characteristics of Votes on Special Rules: 93rd–103rd Congresses

Congress	No. of Roll Calls on Rules Granted	Percentage Consensual (vote > 90%)	Mean Party Difference, Excluding Consensual
93rd (1973-74)	89	44	38
94th (1975-76)	118	60	45
95th (1977-78)	134	56	41
96th (1979-80)	112	52	59
97th (1981-82)	60	30	49
98th (1983-84)	80	21	62
99th (1985-86)	113	27	60
100th (1987-88)	91	13	67
101st (1989-90)	85	18	70
102nd (1991-92)	109	11	80
103rd (1993-94)	84	4	77

Source: David W. Rohde, *Parties and Leaders in the Postreform House* (Chicago: University of Chicago Press, 1991), 102 for 93rd through 100th Congresses and author's calculations for 101st through 103rd Congresses.

the 1970s, beginning in about 1980 that consensus declined. The decline accelerated in the 100th Congress of 1987–88, when Jim Wright exercised his full authority. By the 103rd Congress, almost no rules reported by the Rules Committee gained bipartisan consensus. By this measure, the frequency of support by House Republicans in the structure of House floor deliberations declined from more than half the time to almost never.

The post-reform era saw Republican participation in floor debate restricted to an unprecedented extent. The viability of the strategy to exclude Republicans depended upon Democratic cohesion. Special rules had to attract the support of the vast majority of Democrats since most Republicans opposed restrictions on amendments.[43] One means was through substitutes for the several versions of major bills approved by several committees under the new multiple referral system. Restrictive rules and substitute bills are responses to the possibility that the Committee of the Whole might adopt unwelcome (to the majority leadership) amendments if members could offer them.[44]

Restrictive rules proliferated as their partisan potential became clear. Smith concluded floor rules "often have been motivated by inter-party conflict. . . . The last two decades have shown how the majority party can produce effective procedural change in the majoritarian House [where] developments in the use of the floor frequently have a distinct partisan cast."[45] Republican amendments that might divide Democrats could be avoided by special rules. A majority of House Democrats thought that unfettered amending activity undermining efficiency and threatening party cohesion was an acceptable reason for restrictive floor rules.[46]

A more partisan Rules Committee brought a more partisan response by the House Republicans. During the 1980s more Republican members realized that procedural votes on special rules had enormous policy consequences and that such votes put Republicans at marked political and strategic disadvantages.[47] These handicaps, however, made no headlines. House Republicans objected strenuously to many of the restricted rules, and these objections produced highly partisan voting patterns on special rules. Sometimes rules were blocked, but for the most part large Democratic majorities enabled Democrats to pass rules without Republican support.[48]

Partisan Institutional Change

The House in the post-reform era did not have to evolve into hostile partisanship. Innovations such as leadership task forces and more complex floor voting rules could have been developed in a bipartisan manner and could have enhanced the ability of all members to contribute to policy. Speakers of the House could conceivably have requested the Minority Leader to nominate Republicans to leadership-sanctioned bipartisan task forces to deal with critical issues such as the budget deficit, Central American policy, campaign finance reform, or civil rights. The Rules Committee could have begun to structure rules to ensure that all major points of view on critical legislation were given equal opportunity to be presented on the floor and win majority support. But this did not happen. The institutional trends in Congress from approximately 1978 onward severely diminished the opportunity for minority Republican members to participate in Congress's work in a meaningful way. A primary effect, then, of organizational changes in Congress in the post-reform era was a greater level of policymaking frustration by the minority even as their personal resources and entrepreneurial opportunities expanded.

Informal Entrepreneurial Opportunities

While the legislative and partisan structures of Congress became more rigid, the power of individual members to pursue entrepreneurial activity continued apace. Both Republicans and Democrats had access to more personal assets. These resources made each member more consequential to the leadership—either a more formidable foe or more valuable ally. For the majority, the challenge to Democratic leaders was to keep everyone in line. For the minority, GOP members shunned by the Democrats could cause more trouble.

There are three important areas of new entrepreneurial activity: member resources such as staff and individual office accounts; informal groups and caucuses within the House; and election law changes affecting nominations, elections, and financing.

Personal Member Resources

An individual member of Congress has available up to eighteen full-time and four part-time staff, space for an office in Washington, D.C., and funds for more than one in the district, a personal travel budget, free mailing privileges, advanced computer technology to conduct sophisticated mailing efforts, and various electronic communications abilities. These resources mushroomed in the 1970s and 1980s. Unlike the committee resources discussed above, the historical curve of statistics on personal resources continued its upward climb further into the 1980s. For example, total House personal staff grew from just over 4,000 in 1967 to 6,900 in 1978, peaked at 7,600 in 1983, and stood at 7,500 in 1992.[49]

Statistics on legislative appropriations grew even more regularly. In 1966, it took $198 million to fund the entire legislative branch. By 1976, the legislative budget was $947 million; ten years later that figure had almost doubled to $1.78 billion and rose to $2.3 billion in 1992.[50] Mailing costs and volume were particular areas of growth throughout the last two decades. In 1971, Congress appropriated $11.2 million for congressional franked mail. In 1977, the franked mail appropriation was $47 million, and thirteen years later it was $99 million.[51] Even when these figures are adjusted for postal rate increases, the tide of congressional mail rose consistently. In 1976, 401 million pieces of mail were mailed by representatives and senators, and twelve years later almost exactly twice as many pieces were sent.[52]

But the greatest growth rate has been in member personal office allowances. In 1977, members were allocated $238,000 for staff salaries (their "clerk hire" account), and just under $50,000 for official expenses. Sixteen years later the clerk hire allowance was $557,000, and the official expense allowance ranged from $150,000 to $307,000.[53]

Members of Congress have a wide range of resources that can be devoted to non-legislative activities. Members not interested in or squeezed out of lawmaking can be expected to employ those resources elsewhere, to the possible detriment of the House's lawmaking processes. Traditionally, reelection was the primary interest of members, but the post-reform era brought greater resources and new non-legislative options. Reelection remained a primary concern, but personal advancement within and beyond the electoral process also became important. As a popular management guide for new House members noted:

> At the heart of the current organizational culture of Congress is the notion of the centrality of the individual Member, free to develop an effective, personal organization and pursue personal goals. One senior House Member expressed the idea during new member orientation in 1988: "Congress is like 435 separate corporations."[54]

Even the road to reelection changed course. Higher campaign expenses and a greater share of nonparty campaign funding changed the mix of reelection activities toward more focus on Washington, D.C., and on raising money. More resources were targeted at ideologically-oriented money constituencies that were nationwide rather than geographically isolated.

There are at least two other trends that have redirected resources away from local pork-barreling and constituent casework. First, less federal largesse has meant that the rewards of the pork barrel are available to fewer members. The 1994 congressional elections showed that there may even be incidental (and perhaps growing) negative public reactions against members who are cast as excessively focused on parochial interests. Second, greater personal resources let ideologically inclined members join together to develop policy alternatives. These House members made connections with one another, private interest groups, think tanks, and other entities that have intense interests in ideological issues. For House Republicans, a third trend was their exclusion by the Democratic party leadership. It made sense for Republicans interested in policy to redirect more staff resources—especially resources that had before been used to work in the legislative process—to promote different ideologies and policy alternatives that were not attended to within the partisan House.

Caucus Activity

Legislators complain about single-issue lobbying groups, but they follow the same trend in forming their own groups within Congress.[55] Member groups will undoubtedly continue, despite the decision by the new majority Republicans in the 104th Congress to end funding and the provision of office space for twenty-eight legislative service organizations.

Congress always has contained informal groups. In earlier years these groups focused almost exclusively on state or regional interests, or on personal campaigns for leadership positions. In more recent congresses, however, a greater proportion of groups have been formed around issues of some sort, either single policy issues, broad policy themes or even broader ideological perspectives.[56] In addition, a greater proportion of recently formed groups were organized with the help of outside groups. Among this category of groups are the Steel and Textile Caucuses organized by those industries, and the Republican Study Committee promoted by Washington elites in the New Right movement.[57]

Caucuses mushroomed in the post-reform House, as Hammond has noted. Prior to 1969 there were three caucuses and five years later there were only twelve. By 1980, however, there were about seventy congressional caucuses and by 1987 there were about 120.[58]

Caucus growth apparently reflected attempts to impose order on a disorderly congressional environment, to set the agenda for the House. For House Republicans, the agenda-setting function of caucuses is better seen as an agenda-changing function, for dissatisfaction with the present agenda is a precondition for caucus creation. This Republican agenda-changing function looks outside Congress to alter the *status quo*. This function can be especially useful for all or portions of a House Republican conference shut out of the congressional power structure as they were until 1994.

An initial imperative for an intraparty caucus is to obtain party consideration of "its" issues. In the Republican party each intraparty caucus—the House Wednesday Group, the Republican Study Committee, the Conservative Opportunity Society (COS), and the '92 Group—sought first to influence the House Republican conference.[59] The COS was most successful in setting party agendas, playing the lead role in planning congressional party conferences to discuss emerging issues and the role of the party in the House, and contributing key members to the new more aggressive leadership roster.[60] Individual caucus members created opportunities that included an alternative leadership development arena and a chance to pursue issues outside a member's committee jurisdiction.[61] These opportunities bore increasing fruit as the post-reform era continued.

The mere formation of an intraparty group could be seen as an act of rebellion against established leadership, since these groups usually were organized by members dissatisfied with the way the traditional structures in Congress organized choices and developed agendas.[62] In the Republican party, the House Wednesday Group and the Republican Study Committee were created to embody the views of the party's small liberal wing and the larger conservative wing.[63] To the extent these intraparty groups successfully challenged the established party structures in the post-reform era they kept these structures, such as the Republican Conference, from monopolizing policy leadership.[64] Intraparty caucuses provided alternative power sources.

The proliferation and maintenance of these intraparty groups in the GOP suggest that within the House GOP there are more ideological differences, and more frequent attempts to organize these differences, than usually noted. The decision by the new majority to eliminate the officially sanctioned legislative service organizations is unlikely, by itself, to eliminate dissent within the party or criticism of the new majority by members of either party.

Election-Related Changes

The means by which candidates come forth and campaign has also changed in the past twenty years. The chief effect of electoral changes relevant to this analysis is on the kind of person attracted to congressional service. Open primaries have attracted more policy-based amateurs or entrepreneurs. These "self-starters" tended to be more issue-oriented than other candidates, lending support to the proposition that the composition of Congress has shifted toward a greater number of ideological members.[65] This trend toward entrepreneurial candidacies appears to be a factor in both parties. Local party organizations and national congressional campaign committees now focus on helping self-selected nominees win general elections; very rarely are there successful interventions in nomination fights.

A well-researched aspect of congressional elections is the "incumbency advantage" in which sitting members of Congress have been winning a growing percentage of reelection campaigns, even considering the more tumultuous 1992 and 1994 House elections. Most studies cite the rise of incumbent perquisites for the growing reelection advantage. Other well-known incumbent advantages are name identification, advertising privileges, fundraising, and constituency contact. These and other areas have been discussed at length in a great deal of research.[66] Most of the incumbent advantages accrue to the individual incumbents, and not to their party; i.e., there is a large "personal" incumbent advantage and a small or nonexistent "partisan" incumbent advantage.[67] For the purposes of this study, noting the incumbent advantage points out the increased power individual members have over party leaders. Nonideological members can use this enhanced personal advantage merely to remain in office. More ideological members, however, may use the incumbent advantage to gain greater freedom from party leadership to pursue personal ideologies and issues.

The most easily measured statistics on campaigns are those related to financing. Sources of financing provide further hints about the individualization of congressional campaigns. If a large proportion of funds came from parties, parties could reasonably expect to shape candidate issue content and strategy. Fewer party funds suggest greater candidate independence from parties.

For all candidates and for House Republicans especially, party contributions as a percentage of all contributions have fallen. In 1974 10 percent of House GOP candidate contributions came from PACs, 7 percent from party groups, and 83 percent from individuals or "other" sources. In 1986, the PAC percentage was up to 29, but party spending was only 6 percent. In 1994, House Republicans received 25 percent of their funds from PACs, but only 1 percent from parties.[68] PAC contributions as a percentage of all contributions have risen to about one-fourth to one-third of contributions to House Republicans, while party contributions have not increased at all over twenty years. Party money has no more, and almost certainly less, influence over members today than twenty years ago.

How party nominees are selected also affects party discipline. James Thurber found that "party involvement in the recruitment process is an important factor"[69] in explaining a legislator's partisan actions in office. The greater a party's influence in nominee selection, the more likely a nominee, once elected, will vote the party line. Steven Haeberle found that "members of Congress with the highest levels of party support in the House of Representatives are elected in states using closed primaries,"[70] rather than open or blanket primaries, suggesting that strong state party systems encourage national party loyalty. Both Thurber and Haeberle emphasized the strong positive correlation between party influence in candidate selection and election, and later vote conformity in the House.

Financial and issue assistance induces representatives to be more ideologically in tune with the sources of that assistance once in office. In the late 1970s and early 1980s, the National Republican Campaign Committee (NRCC) became more involved in campaign aid. Paul Herrnson found that the national congressional campaign committees of both parties provided candidates with technical and issue-related assistance, but that Republicans provided more of each type of assistance to both challengers and incumbents.[71] The National Republican Congressional Committee (NRCC) also coordinated so-called "independent" PAC contributions to Republicans. Herrnson noted that in the 1984 election cycle the NRCC "designed the PAC solicitation strategies of about 100 Republican contenders. . . . The committee arranged for small meetings to take place between these candidates and leading members of the PAC community. It also helped to design 'PAC-Kits' the candidates used to solicit PAC contributions."[72] Republicans reported more management, communications, issues, and fundraising assistance from the NRCC than Democrats reported from the

DCCC; and Republican incumbents used all these services at higher levels than incumbent Democrats.[73]

In the latter years of the post-reform era, the direct influence of the NRCC in congressional elections diminished. For many candidates for the House, the NRCC became secondary in time and effect to GOPAC, led for most of that time by Newt Gingrich. Sensing a need to recruit and train Republicans far earlier than general elections for the U.S. House, GOPAC encouraged Republicans to run for local and state offices and taught them how to run, win, and get reelected. After Gingrich took the helm of GOPAC in the mid-1980s, the organization invested a great deal of resources in developing qualified candidates, many of whom were to become experienced elected officials in state and local governments. Many of these GOPAC-trained officials, in turn, could be expected eventually to seek higher offices, including seats in the House. By the late 1980s the GOPAC strategy was bearing fruit in creating a larger pool of qualified House GOP candidates.

Another election financing strategy outside the NRCC grew up alongside GOPAC's efforts. Incumbent Republicans (especially current or aspiring leaders) began to contribute to key challenger or open-seat candidates out of their own campaign committees or separate leadership PACs. The NRCC would identify opportunities and encourage current House Republicans to contribute to these key races. While incumbents seeking freshman support in leadership races were the most likely to adopt this strategy, the NRCC urged all members to participate in order to receive timely cash infusions in key races.

This new strategy proved effective in two May 1994 races for open seats in Oklahoma and Kentucky. Both districts were conservative but had two-to-one Democratic voter registration advantages and had been represented by Democrats for decades. These natural Democratic advantages were overcome by anti-Clinton campaign rhetoric recommended by the NRCC and large infusions of campaign funds directed, but not financed, by the campaign committee. In the Kentucky race, Republican winner Ron Lewis received about $200,000 in the last weeks of his campaign, much of it contributed by incumbent House Republicans seeking to claim an upset victory.[74] The experience of these two races taught Republicans the value of this new strategy, which was to be implemented on a much grander scale in the fall.

The 1994 elections showed how successful the strategy of complementing direct NRCC efforts with additional Republican support could be. Thirty-three out of the seventy-three new House Republicans were large and direct beneficiaries of GOPAC efforts, and most others could point to the influence of GOPAC in their successful congressional efforts.[75] And almost all incoming freshmen received timely donations, campaign tips, or other kinds of assistance from all incumbent Republicans in leadership races, and even many members in the GOP rank and file.[76] The NRCC had successfully moved from providing direct campaign advice and funds, to serving as a catalyst for more timely and effective Republican-dominated campaign resources.

Partisan Campaign Consequences

Many scholars have noted the greater "complexity" of Congress as individual resources grew and institutional structures expanded. Less noted is the partisan aspect of this greater complexity. In order to fulfill Congress's legislative role, floor majorities must develop. Greater member independence in both parties and greater ideological influence within the Republican party induced Democratic party leaders (while they were in the majority) to restrict the arena of majority vote building from the Congress as a whole to the Democratic Caucus. Once the trends toward partisanship began, it was easier to develop a working majority within one party than across the two parties. As California Democrat Henry Waxman noted, "[i]f we have a united Democratic position, Republicans are irrelevant."[77] Partisanship, which began to assert itself in the mid-1970s, seemed to feed on itself during the 1980s and early 1990s. Over time, GOP participation in the traditional legislative work of the House diminished to virtually nothing.

One clear indication of declining GOP influence in the House is the "money trail" of PAC contributions. Political action committees are sophisticated investors in lawmaking, by their contributions seeking influence with key lawmakers at key points in the legislative process. Members of Congress with great power in the process can expect a large number of PAC contributions; those with little power can expect few contributions. PAC contributions can also be highly sensitive to changes in power relationships, as they are made voluntarily, at any time, usually by PAC directors trained to most effectively time their contributions.

PAC contributions in the post-reform era show a growing concentration among Democrats, parallel to the restrictions their party leaders made on committee and floor debate. This concentration is true for contributions from all kinds of PACs, even corporate PACs that could be expected to give predominantly to pro-business Republicans.

While the conventional wisdom is that both parties, or even perhaps primarily the Republican party, benefit from special interest financing, the statistics of the post-reform era indicate otherwise. Especially in the early and mid-1980s, Democrats were able to concentrate PAC giving in their own party.

The overall partisan pattern of PAC financing in House races changed dramatically from 1978 through 1994.[78] Republican receipts grew quickly in the first few elections but then leveled off. In 1978, Republican receipts from PACs totaled about $22 million (in 1994 constant dollars) for all races, about 17 percent of funds. The amount rose to $39 million in 1982 and the percentage to 25. Since then, the amount has held roughly constant at $40 million, and the percentage has been in the middle to upper 20s.

Democrats enjoyed a steady rise in amount and percentage of PAC receipts in the post-reform era. In 1978, Democrats received about $25 million in PAC contributions, about 27 percent of all campaign funds. Four years later, Democrats received almost exactly twice the amount, which constituted about one-third of all Democratic receipts. From 1982 through 1988, PAC contributions to Democrats rose about $10 million per election cycle when they reached the current plateau of about $80 million. As a percentage of funds, PAC contributions were above 40 percent of aggregate Democratic candidate funds every election year since 1984, and approached half of all party candidate funds in 1988 and 1990.

The amount PACs contribute to challengers is also important. Most federal PACs have close connections to the Washington power centers, whether or not the PACs have headquarters in the area. PAC contributions to challengers are thus influenced by the power of incumbents, as these incumbents can guide PAC contributions to friends and away from enemies. Challengers from the "right" party can easily get PAC funds, while challengers from the "wrong" party will find few PACs willing to give to them and risk the wrath of the party in power.

As Democrats consolidated power PAC contributions to GOP challengers fell. In 1982, Republican challengers received 17 percent of all their campaign funds from PACs, while Democratic challengers received 28 percent. Between 1982 and 1986, the Republican percentage was cut nearly in half, and it has remained between 9 and 11 percent of funds through 1994. But the Democratic percentage grew to range between the high 20s and low 30s.

Corporate political action committees typically seek to defend and expand the access business has to the legislative process, and their basic interests in favor of freer markets are consistent with the views of Republicans. But corporate PACs are also "pragmatic" in that they seek to maintain good relations with whomever holds power. As such, the pattern of corporate PAC contributions can reveal who holds real power in the House. In the early years, the percentage of corporate PAC funds to Republicans was fairly high, especially in 1980 and 1982 when House Republicans appeared to be ascending in power and might have become the majority with one or two more favorable elections. The 1982 elections, however, broke the GOP momentum and corporate PAC contributions declined in turn. Peaking at 63 percent in 1982, the percentage of corporate PAC funds going to Republicans fell to about 50 percent four years later, and down to 45 percent in 1992 and 1994. Vocally opposed to most of their agenda, Democratic leaders still got corporations to give Democrats the majority of corporate PAC funds.

Another way information on PAC receipts can reveal the distribution of power in the House is the partisan split of top PAC recipients. Here, the bias is overwhelming, with Democrats pulling ahead in 1982 and quickly dominating, if not monopolizing, the number of top PAC recipients. In 1980, for example, the top fifty, twenty-five, and ten PAC recipients included an approximately equal number of Republicans and Democrats. Two years later, the Democratic proportion rose to about two-thirds. Six years after that, in 1988, Democrats composed almost 90 percent of all three categories, a proportion that held through the 1994 elections. Clearly, Republicans sought to devise new campaign

TABLE 2.4
Democratic Proportion of Top PAC Recipients: 1980–1994

Election Year	Top 50 (Percent Democratic)	Top 25 (Percent Democratic)	Top 10 (Percent Democratic)
1980	48	48	60
1982	62	64	80
1984	82	88	80
1986	72	80	90
1988	88	88	90
1990	90	92	100
1992	90	92	90
1994	94	92	90

Source: Federal Elections Commission

techniques such as GOPAC involvement in nonfederal campaigns and NRCC activity in coordinating leadership and incumbent giving, in order to channel adequate funds to quality Republican open-seat and challenger candidates who would not otherwise receive funds from cautious and cowed political action committees.

Conclusion

The concentration of power in the Democratic party makes it less appropriate to try to identify intraparty factions by voting analysis. Greater partisanship made Republicans vote like a more cohesive party, an effect borne out by traditional measures of cohesion that were at historically high levels in the early 1990s. The GOP voted together to oppose what was often perceived as majority tyranny exercised through floor rules and other procedures.[79]

The entrepreneurial connection to outside interests, however, simultaneously made the post-reform House GOP think less cohesively when measures of ideology and institutional attitudes are used. Greater individual freedom and resources encouraged policy-oriented Republicans to look for mutual support inside and outside of Congress, beyond traditional party organs. Hence, there was an increase in the number and size of intraparty and personal interest caucuses, and more connections among these groups and outside interest groups and think tanks. The consequence was ideological factionalism in the House GOP, and greater durability of these factions over time and across issues.

The partisan aspects of congressional change have been pointed out and the consequences of these changes on the GOP have been discussed. The next step is to review the various outside ideological movements around which increasingly alienated and entrepreneurial House Republicans gathered.

Notes

1. See, for example, the relevant chapters on norms in Barbara Hinckley, *Stability and Change in Congress*, 4th ed. (New York: Harper and Row, 1988), and Edward V. Schneier and Bertram Gross, *Congress Today* (New York: St. Martin's Press, 1993).

2. The authors cited in the previous footnote give slightly different names

to the first norm. Hinckley emphasizes the power of senior members by labeling it seniority; Schneier and Gross emphasize junior members and label it apprenticeship, the flip side of the same coin.

3. Richard Cohen, "Gingrich: From Gadfly to Whip," *National Journal* 21 (25 March 1989): 743.

4. William F. Connelly, Jr., and John J. Pitney, Jr. *Congress' Permanent Minority?: Republicans in the U.S. House* (Lanham, Md.: Rowman & Littlefield, 1994), 77–79.

5. *Congressional Record*, daily ed., 29 March 1990, H1254.

6. Norman J. Ornstein, Thomas E. Mann, and Michael J. Malbin, *Vital Statistics on Congress: 1993–1994* (Washington, D.C.: Congressional Quarterly, 1994), 114. The number fell to 115 in 1994 under the Democrats in response to reform pressures, and fell all the way to under ninety in the 104th Congress.

7. Ornstein, *Vital Statistics*, 114.

8. Ornstein, *Vital Statistics*, 132.

9. An exception is Roger Davidson, *The Postreform Congress* (New York: St. Martin's Press, 1992), which notes in its preface the same timing problem mentioned here, on p. vii.

10. Richard F. Fenno, Jr., "The Internal Distribution of Influence: The House," in *Readings on Congress*, ed. Raymond E. Wolfinger (Englewood Cliffs, N.J.: Prentice-Hall, 1971).

11. Fenno, "Internal Distribution," 218.

12. Harvey Mansfield, Sr., "The Dispersion of Authority in Congress," in *Congress Against the Presidency* (New York: Academy of Political Science, 1975), 1–19.

13. Mansfield, 18.

14. Mansfield, 19.

15. Lawrence C. Dodd, and Bruce I. Oppenheimer, "Consolidating Power in the House," in *Congress Reconsidered*, 4th ed., ed. Dodd and Oppenheimer (Washington, D.C.: Congressional Quarterly Press, 1989), 48–49.

16. Hinckley, *Stability and Change*, 175.

17. Ornstein, *Vital Statistics*, 201–5, and Kitty Cunningham, "With Democrat in White House, Partisanship Hits New High," *Congressional Quarterly Weekly Report* 51 (18 December 1993): 3432–34.

18. Ornstein, *Vital Statistics*, 203, and Bob Benenson, "Clinton Keeps Southern Wing on His Team in 1993," *Congressional Quarterly Weekly Report* 51 (18 December 1993): 3435–38.

19. Barbara Sinclair, "Majority Party Leadership Strategies For Coping With the New U.S. House," *Legislative Studies Quarterly* 6 (1981): 391.

20. Sinclair, "Majority Party Leadership," 392.

21. Barbara Sinclair, "The Speaker's Task Force in the Post-Reform House of Representatives," *American Political Science Review* 75 (1981): 397–410.

22. Sinclair, "The Speaker's Task Force," 397.

23. Sinclair, "The Speaker's Task Force," 399.

24. Sinclair, "The Speaker's Task Force," 409.

25. Burdett Loomis, "Congressional Careers and Party Leadership in the Contemporary House of Representatives," *American Journal of Political Science* 28 (1984): 196.

26. Loomis, 185.

27. Loomis, 186.

28. Loomis, 190.

29. Charles Tiefer and Hyde Murray, "Congressional Elites Become Take-Charge Managers in a New Era," *Legal Times*, 18 September 1982, 38.

30. Barbara Sinclair, "House Majority Party Leadership in an Era of Divided Control," in *Congress Reconsidered*, 5th ed., ed. Lawrence C. Dodd and Bruce I. Oppenheimer (Washington, D.C.: Congressional Quarterly Press, 1994).

31. Sinclair, "House Majority Party Leadership," 241.

32. Stanley Bach and Steven S. Smith, *Managing Uncertainty in the House of Representatives* (Washington, D.C.: Brookings Institution, 1988), 44.

33. Ornstein, *Vital Statistics*, 153–54.

34. Ornstein, *Vital Statistics*, 157.

35. Ornstein, *Vital Statistics*, 180.

36. Bach, 50.

37. Bach, 51.

38. Congress, House, Committee on Rules, *Rules Committee Calendars and Surveys of Activities*, 95th–102nd Congresses: "Notices of Actions Taken," 103rd Congress, 1st session.

39. Bach, 57.

40. Steven S. Smith, "Taking It to the Floor," in *Congress Reconsidered*, 4th ed., ed. Lawrence C. Dodd and Bruce I. Oppenheimer (Washington, D.C.: Congressional Quarterly Press, 1989), 334.

41. Tiefer, 38.

42. Bach, 37.

43. Steven S. Smith, *Call to Order: Floor Politics in the House and Senate* (Washington, D.C.: Brookings Institution, 1989), 42.

44. Smith, *Call To Order*, 68.

45. Smith, "Taking It," 335.

46. Smith, "Taking It," 347.

47. Bach, 91.

48. Smith, "Taking It," 341.

49. Ornstein, *Vital Statistics*, 126.

50. Ornstein, *Vital Statistics*, 138–39.

51. Ornstein, *Vital Statistics*, 143.

52. Ornstein, *Vital Statistics*, 163.

53. Ornstein, *Vital Statistics*, 144.

54. Craig Schultz, ed., *Setting Course: A Congressional Management Guide* (Washington, D.C.: Congressional Management Foundation, 1994), 8.

55. Roger B. Davidson and Walter Oleszek, *Congress and Its Members* (Washington, D.C.: Congressional Quarterly Press, 1981), 352.

56. Davidson and Oleszek, *Congress and Its Members* (1981), 352.

57. Davidson and Oleszek, *Congress and Its Members* (1981), 352, and Paul Gottfried and Thomas Fleming, *The Conservative Movement* (Boston: Twayne Publishers, 1988), 79.

58. Susan Webb Hammond, "Congressional Caucuses in the Policy Process," *Congress Reconsidered*, 4th ed., ed. Lawrence C. Dodd and Bruce I. Oppenheimer (1989), 351–71.

59. For a history of the Republican Study Committee see Edwin J. Feulner, Jr., *Conservatives Stalk the House: The Story of the Republican Study Committee, 1970–1982* (Ottawa, Ill.: Green Hill Press, 1983). For a study of the Wednesday Group see Robert L. Peabody, "The Ford-Halleck Minority Leadership Contest, 1965," in *Leadership in Congress* (Boston: Little, Brown, 1976). A review of the Conservative Opportunity Society is in "The Conservative Opportunity Society: New Directions, New Leaders for the GOP?" *Conservative Digest*, August 1984. The '92 Group is discussed in Nicol Rae, *The Decline and Fall of Liberal Republicans: 1952 to the Present* (New York: Oxford University Press, 1989).

60. Hammond, "Caucuses in the Policy Process," 362.

61. Hammond, "Caucuses in the Policy Process," 365.

62. Stevens, 426.

63. Stevens, 427.

64. Stevens, 427.

65. Thomas E. Mann, "Elections and Change in Congress," in *The New Congress*, ed. Norman Ornstein (Washington, D.C.: American Enterprise Institute, 1981), 38.

66. See, for example, Hinckley, *Stability and Change*, 46–51.

67. John R. Alford and David W. Brady, "Personal and Partisan Advantage in U.S. Congressional Elections," in *Congress Reconsidered*, 5th ed., ed. Lawrence C. Dodd and Bruce I. Oppenheimer (Washington, D.C.: Congressional Quarterly Press, 1994).

68. Ornstein, *Vital Statistics*, 85.

69. James A. Thurber, "The Impact of Party Recruitment Activity Upon Legislative Role Orientations: A Path Analysis," *Legislative Studies Quarterly* 1 (1976): 546.

70. Steven H. Haeberle, "Closed Primaries and Party Support in Congress," *American Politics Quarterly* 13 (1985): 341–52.

71. Paul S. Herrnson, "Do Parties Make a Difference? The Role of Party Organizations in Congressional Elections," *Journal of Politics* 48 (1986): 589–615.

72. Herrnson, 593.

73. Herrnson, 601–5.

74. Collette Gergely, "GOP Wins Second Special Election in Two Weeks," *Congressional Quarterly Weekly Report* 52 (28 May 1994): 1410.

75. Stephen Engelberg and Katharine Q. Seelye, "Gingrich: Man in Spotlight and Organization in Shadow," *New York Times*, 18 December 1994, A1, 32.

76. Catalina Camia, "Some Republican Contests May Hinge on Freshmen," *Congressional Quarterly Weekly Report* 52 (19 November 1994): 3329.

77. Janet Hook, "House GOP: Plight of a Permanent Minority," *Congressional Quarterly Weekly Report* 44 (June 21, 1986): 1393.

78. Except where specifically indicated, the data in this section come from the Federal Elections Committee in regularly published reports, especially "Congressional Fundraising Information" (Washington, D.C.) from various years.

79. See, for example, Richard Cowan, "The Money Pit," *American Politics* 3 (1988): 10–17; Norman Ornstein, "Minority Report," *Atlantic Monthly*, December 1985, 30, 32, 35, 36, 38; and Bill Whalen, "Ruling the House the Wright Way," *Insight*, 6 February 1989, 24–25.

Chapter 3

Changes in Representation and Ideology Within the House Republican Conference

Chapter two showed how the post-reform Democratic House grew in partisanship, and how it differed from earlier congresses in the structure of incentives influencing members, groups, and parties. Republicans felt these influences differently from Democrats and changed their behaviors and roles.

Generally, political scientists describe two roles that a representative plays on substantive issues—delegate or trustee. A delegate attempts to discover and follow the wishes of his or her constituents. A trustee attempts to serve the long-term interest of his or her constituents, with less regard to their immediate views. Members of Congress tend either to be delegates or trustees. Many combine these roles, and the same member may act as a delegate in one situation and a trustee in another.[1]

These concepts are helpful tools in analysis. Either role, however, is problematic. Delegates face the difficulty of discovering the wishes of their constituents, encountering uncertainty, ignorance, and conflicting demands among voters. Trustees face problems of defining the precise constituency one is working in the best interest of, as well as knowing what constitutes the "best" interest on an issue.

In spite of these problems, the theoretical separation between delegate and trustee roles suggests helpful distinctions among House Republicans. This analysis connects these theoretical roles with measurable activities. It assumes that delegates are more oriented toward local concerns; spend more time consulting local constituencies; and are less ideologically, policy, and party oriented. The delegate orientation is exhibited in fewer memberships on policy committees, party committees, and intraparty groups. It may also be exhibited in more memberships in constituency-based caucuses and seats on constitu-

61

ency committees. Delegates also have lower activity scores, and the
activity that is measured is directed toward constituency interests.
Trustees tend to be more involved in policy and influence committees,
party committees, and issue-based caucuses and informal groups.
Trustees have higher activity levels which can be directed in various
ways, but most likely in the partisan and policy arenas. The approach
taken here estimates the intensity and content of each House Republican's activity in either the local/delegate or national/trustee direction,
based on data about each representative's behavior. High levels of
trustee behavior and low levels of delegate behavior indicate policy-
oriented members; little trustee behavior and significant delegate behavior indicate constituency-oriented members.

Entrepreneurial Members and Their Differing Goals

Entrepreneurial members may have both individual goals for personal
advancement, and group goals for the advancement of the party or
institution. For the majority party the personal and group interests are
often related. Majority members can advance personal goals through a
legislature with reliable norms that help it to work effectively. In
fact, ambitious majority party legislators will seek to protect the
institution's prestige for both personal and party purposes.

For minority members, however, institutional and individual interests are more often distinct. A. James Reichley's distinction between
positional and ideological conservatism clarifies this distinction around
issues, but is also helpful in thinking about institutional norms.[2] Positional conservatism, tied to tradition, seeks to delay outcomes in
whatever direction change is going. Ideological conservatism reflects
on the framework of policy. It may seek to slow change, but more
likely its goal is to alter the outcome and agenda. Positionally conservative House GOP members believe that individual and institutional
interests still converge. They will thus defend the old norms, while
opposing some Democratic policies along the way. Policy-oriented
ideological House Republicans behave differently. They believe individual and institutional interests often conflict. Thus, they often attack
congressional norms as working against their individual goals. These
different assessments of congressional norms also create conflict
within the party.

Because norms are largely formed by the majority, minority acquiescence to norms may indicate lack of minority resolve. Ideological
conservatives can often oppose positional ones over norms. Some-

times it can appear that positional conservatives line up with programmatic liberals.[3] After World War II, for example, Congress and the president were ideologically liberal—united in support of the New Deal and its basic assumption of a competent, growing national government. Congress was usually positionally conservative compared with presidents, and there were few ideological conservatives in the House. Conversely, post-reform Democrats were ideologically liberal, but positionally conservative when it came to adopting supply-side economics or overturning decisions of the Warren-led Supreme Court. While in the majority, these Democrats often found allies among positionally conservative Republicans, unnerving more ideologically conservative Republican members.

Junior House Republicans may also be more ideological and entrepreneurial because of their route to the House. Many younger entrepreneurs came from religious and populist ranks, often recruited by GOPAC. Once elected to the House, they were nurtured by New Right groups in Washington or Christian Coalition members at the grassroots. In the post-reform House, these entrepreneurs converged around ideologically oriented or personal goal-oriented factions within the House Republican party, not around the party itself. These new convergences appear most clearly in intraparty groups that rejected the attitudes or positions of the older minority-party order. The most prominent of these groups was the Conservative Opportunity Society, but in muted form, the '92 Group also worked against the old party order.

Increased ideologically oriented group activity outside party channels clashes with the definition of responsible party government in the 1950 APSA report. Caucuses and intraparty groups advance narrower interests or more extreme points of view, which conflict with the preferred tradition of broadly based and programmatic parties.

The goal of the report's authors was to encourage a party responsibility that had little ideological content. The majority party was to be responsible for agenda setting and for pushing that agenda through the executive and legislative branches. In the legislature, the report argued, the majority party should set the scope of accepted debate and promote legislative ideas within that scope; the minority should present alternative legislative ideas within the boundaries set by the majority. Responsible two-party discipline meant two things to writers of the report—responsibility within the majority to set a program, and discipline within the members of both parties to abide by that agenda. Fundamental disagreement about the ends of government had little place in the theory.

While this view of party responsibility is popular, an alternative view is needed to interpret correctly the post-reform era and the changes brought by a House Republican majority. As Michael J. Malbin has noted, the type of two-party discipline envisioned by the writers of the 1950 report presupposed either a nation far less diverse than the United States in which parties are little more than organizational conveniences, or a nation so polarized by divisive issues that voters are willing to accept limited choices.[4] The alternative theory begins with a starkly different view of the legitimate range of public debate. As Malbin implies, the responsible two-party model supposes an electorate and elite either overwhelmingly pragmatic, or a public so polarized along a fixed unidimensional ideological spectrum that either/ or choices reflect policy options. Scholars have tended to desire the clear choices the latter offers while decrying that the former, with party "irresponsibility," seems prevalent.

Increased Ideological Influence

Congress in the post-reform era grew to differ from the largely pragmatic and programmatic House viewed by the APSA report writers. While GOP representatives in the post-reform era remained primarily pragmatic, many of them came from ideological movements, and all of them were influenced by the greater ideological conservatism of Reagan Republicanism. The ideological elements of the broader Reagan "movement" wanted not only to affect items on the New Deal agenda, but to change the agenda itself.

New political ideas caused at least two cleavages among House Republicans. The first was a substantive difference on whether greater ideological debate would help the party. The second was a strategic difference whether to emphasize old tactics or new ideas. The utility of Reiter's terminology of "regulars," "realigners," and "misfits" is especially apparent during this time of ideological ferment and partisan disruption.

There are many consequences to this greater ideological content of congressional debate. The chief consequence this analysis examines is the greater tendency for legislators to organize around distinct sets of ideas.

Ideology in Congress

It is appropriate at this point to describe the "dominant Democratic framework" against which conservative thought and Republican activity have grappled. "New Deal," "Great Society," and "liberal" have been used so far with little elaboration. The shift from the New Deal consensus during the 1970s becomes clearer if a distinction is made between the *framework* of policymaking and the *outcome* of legislative bargaining.

The "dominant Democratic framework" is that set of positions on economic, social, and foreign policy legislation taken by the bulk of congressional Democrats from the mid-1970s to the present. This definition incorporates that party's post-Vietnam reaction against military action and post-Watergate response against government secrecy, together with the drive for more equal distribution of material goods. This definition differs slightly from New Deal/Great Society policies of earlier Democrats. Presidents Franklin Roosevelt and Lyndon Johnson combined an expansive domestic agenda with an assertive international policy. Since the late 1960s, however, an aggressive foreign policy has been a minority voice in the Democratic party. Democratic party internationalists since then have been advocating abstract human rights, supporting the United Nations and other international bureaucracies, and hesitating to use military force.

Both Congress and presidents in the New Deal and Great Society eras operated in the policy *framework* of intervention and centralization. Presidents generally wanted to travel more quickly down that road while Congress wanted to go more slowly. Both, however, accepted the presumption to travel down the same road. Disputes between Congress and the president were really incremental disagreements about interim outcomes.

Most congressional studies missed the provisional nature of that framework. Traditional means of resolving or muting congressional conflict—bargaining among committee chairs and ranking members or majority- and minority-party leaders, back-room dealing, log-rolling, teller or voice voting, an open floor process and other measures—all worked well in an era of bipartisan pragmatism traveling the same path. None, however, works well in a fragmented entrepreneurial environment with deeper ideological divisions. Disputes have increasingly occurred over ideas, not appropriations.

The analysis so far indicates why studies of floor votes are inadequate to describe the complexity in the House GOP—they simply do not explain major conflicts among minority party members over issues such as ideology, representational styles, and attitudes toward congressional norms.

Past Studies of Congressional Republicans

As noted earlier, Reichley studied Republicans in both the executive and legislative branches during the early 1970s. He categorized elites and rank and file as Fundamentalists, Stalwarts, Moderates, and Progressives. Fundamentalists were the most conservative GOP faction. During the Nixon-Ford era, Fundamentalists were relatively new to the party, more ideological than long-term Republicans. White southerners and Roman Catholics were the two major Fundamentalist elements at the grassroots. Fundamentalists supported American military supremacy, either to protect military and economic interests or to aid a global crusade for democratic capitalism against communism. Most Fundamentalists agreed on the foreign policy agenda, but their energy was directed to domestic issues like drugs, crime, racial tensions (in opposition to aggressive integration), and sexual morality. Reichley noted that Fundamentalists split on the size and scope of government—some opposed domestic government programs as interfering with the American family while others encouraged them because they might allow economically pressured families to remain together. Fundamentalists were prevalent in the Sunbelt and in rural regions of the Rocky Mountains and Great Plains. The key personality associated with Fundamentalists was Barry Goldwater, especially during the 1964 campaign. In the 1968 Republican presidential primaries, Reichley found that Fundamentalists were divided between citizen activists who tended to support Ronald Reagan, and professional politicians such as John Tower of Texas and Strom Thurmond of South Carolina who supported Nixon.

The Fundamentalist faction contained cross-pressured groups that have since parted ways. The first split has come over the two reasons for military supremacy, which somewhat awkwardly coexisted in the 1960s and 1970s—to preserve American values at home and to promulgate them around the world. With the end of the Cold War, this split between isolationists and internationalists will continue unless and until new common enemies emerge. A second new split is between the "libertarian" and the "moralist" over government action toward social or moral issues. United against liberal social policy, the more libertarian elements would prefer government retreat, while moralists would prefer government-led redirection to enforce conservative social positions.

Reichley's second faction, the Stalwarts, constituted the backbone of the party. They rose from small-town, middle-class Protestant society, especially the middle-sized cities of the Midwest. Stalwarts professed reverence for the Constitution and the American economic system. Loyalty to the party and these principles were Stalwart trademarks. Stalwarts were also more sympathetic to "Main Street" than to "Wall Street." As such, Stalwarts could rationalize antimonopoly legislation and certain tariff protection. Domestically, Stalwarts were positional conservatives, seeking to slow the rate of change rather than to reverse its direction. Stalwarts were part of the GOP history of progressive treatment of minorities, and generally supported early civil rights legislation. In foreign policy, however, Stalwarts were divided between isolationists and internationalists. Stalwarts included Robert Taft, Gerald Ford, and Everett Dirksen. Headquartered in the heartland, Stalwarts also drew support from upstate Pennsylvania; upstate New York and some of New England; and parts of Florida, Texas, and California where the GOP had been established for some time. Under pressure from Reagan foreign policy, the isolationist versus internationalist division within the Stalwarts has become more apparent, with isolationists (centered in the Plains states) less comfortable with the Reagan foreign policy agenda.

Reichley's third group was Moderates, identified with Easterners Thomas Dewey, Henry Cabot Lodge, Jr., and Hugh Scott. Moderates were content to manage the settled New Deal agenda. In foreign policy, Moderates were internationalists, intent to pursue the tangible benefits of foreign investment and free trade (the interests of corporate business) more than the idealistic rewards of extending democratic capitalism or preserving a nation of shopkeepers. Moderates represented corporate bedroom suburbs of major urban areas across the North. Although Moderates had little apparent cohesiveness underpinning their me-too-ism and pragmatism, they had none of the cross-pressures faced by the Fundamentalist and Stalwart camps.

Reichley's final group was Progressives. This group traced its origins to Lincoln's governmental activism and Theodore Roosevelt's zest for social reform. Progressives nearly died out as a party force after Theodore Roosevelt's bolt from the party in 1912; however, the progressive strain of Republicanism was resurrected for a time by Nelson Rockefeller in his election as New York governor in 1958. In the 1960s and later, Progressive ideas were embodied in a small group of senators including Jacob Javits, Charles Percy, Mark Hatfield, and Edward Brooke. Progressives believed that the way to win the presidency was to match or exceed the Democrats' perceived commitment to meeting public needs. Progressives, however, thought the first step in that strategy was to complement and encourage private enterprise. The Progressives were also responsive to the national media and to intellectual trends and agendas, reflecting their strong ties to media centers in the East and eastern Midwest, and their elevated educational and socioeconomic position.

In the years since Reichley's description, the Progressive faction has shrunk significantly. It does not appear to be in danger of petering out, however, as new GOP representatives continue to be elected from traditional GOP districts in New England and Mid-Atlantic states. Clearly, however, Progressives remain tenuously attached to the GOP.

Recent Developments in the House GOP

Reichley's descriptions are vivid but dated as new events and ideological movements have changed the shape of the Republican coalition. An initial step in exploring the complexity of House Republicans in this more ideological and entrepreneurial time is to examine conservative attacks on the New Deal/Great Society consensus. Particular attention is paid to developments in the conservative movement and what is usually labeled "conservative" thought because national Republicans—except for a few persons in the Northeast—tend to accept that label (even though the terms "liberal" and "conservative" have lost much of their utility in describing American politics).

Just how many conservative strains exist is a subject of debate. Some writers see American conservatism as a single entity competing with and complementing liberalism as the dominant American view. Others identify two conservative strains of varying origin. There is the "Old Right" versus "New Right" division, based primarily on the age and energy of the adherents.[5] Another bipolar division similar to the one Reichley notes is a "paternalistic" conservatism that accepts the basic premises of modern liberalism, vying against a libertarian conservatism that supports free-market economics but traditional social authority. Still others see three strains: religious conservatism, libertarian conservatism, and traditional paternalistic conservatism.[6] Paul Gottfried and Thomas Fleming found four ideological conservative responses to the dominant Democratic framework, which joined one lone strand of traditional Old Right conservatism.[7] The four ideological influences were the religious right, the populist New Right, libertarians, and neoconservatives. This five-part division of modern American conservatism, with only one traditional strand, is open to debate. For example, a libertarian-like stream affiliated with Robert Taft-era isolationism and anti-New Dealism has long historical GOP ties. Gottfried and Fleming date libertarianism later than Taft's influence in the party and closer to the stream of supply-side economics than many others would. Despite a few minor problems, however, Gottfried and Fleming's division helps identify the widest range of ideological influences in today's Republican party.

The Republican party, especially in its weakened condition after Watergate, was the logical vehicle for conservative activists from varied ideological camps. And it was in Congress, an institution with no power to choose its members, and in local parties, with dwindling influence over their nominees and even their own community activists, where these new elements most easily gained office. With member turnover, these new elements began to share the conservative and Republican labels with more traditional views and elites from different backgrounds. The old and new elements formed a more complex conservatism that now defines congressional Republican politics.

The Religious Right

The religious right is not the same as the New Right.[8] The former is a narrowly focused but key grassroots element of a complex antigovernment movement. New Rightists are more experienced at the elite level and more active across a far wider range of issues.

Religious conservatives came late to political activism, asserting major influence only after the mid-1970s. Before then, a wide range of religious conservatives—chiefly evangelicals, religious Fundamentalists, and rural and ethnic elements of traditional Protestant denominations—usually operated comfortably within an American polity built on a civil religion rooted in the Puritanism of colonial America.[9] These apolitical groups held a vision of a society whose citizens professed faith in God and country, whose laws encouraged public morality, and whose leaders espoused mainstream American values. Legal and political support of that society came from federal and state laws protecting prayer in schools, permitting other religious influences in public education, restricting abortion, limiting income redistribution, and preferring traditional family arrangements over alternative lifestyles.

By the mid-1970s, however, many traditional religious leaders began to believe that national government institutions were corroding American values. The chief offender was the judiciary—particularly the

Supreme Court under Chief Justice Earl Warren and, specifically the *Roe v. Wade* abortion decision. Also at fault were Great Society congresses that channeled federal dollars to "suspect" groups. A growing number of religious conservatives began to view political action as necessary to revive traditional values and reverse government-supported secularization.

These religious rightists entered politics in the mid-1970s. Their anger was expressed in a mix of ideological and positional conservative language attacking what they perceived to be excessive secularism. Tim LaHaye, a major leader of the Christian Right complained that secular "humanism . . . has moved our country from a biblically based society to an amoral 'democratic' society during the past forty years."[10] The strategy for religious conservatives was to roll back new judicial and legislative decisions to restore a particular religious vision of America—an ideological stance demanding aggressive political action. But the motivation was more positional—a longing for a previous vision of a pastoral society where unwritten norms of behavior reinforced wholesome values and obviated the need for government interference.

This mix of positional and ideological conservatism tied religious traditionalists to old Republicanism as well as new ideological streams. Whereas the political energy required to accomplish the goals of the religious right fit the activism of the ideological New Right and neoconservatives, the religious right's vision was closer to that of positional conservatives.

Another distinguishing characteristic of the religious right until the late 1980s was its narrow political agenda. From its start in the mid-1970s through at least the late 1980s, it focused on a few domestic issues such as abortion, personal lifestyles, and the support of religious values in education. There is no fixed connection between these issues and economics or national security. Religious rightists can be populist or conservative in other domestic matters and isolationist, internationalist, or militarist in foreign policy.[11]

The narrow religious conservative agenda has changed in recent years, at least at the elite level. The presidential campaign of Pat Robertson in 1988 helped organize religious conservatives across a broader issue spectrum as the candidate had to take stands across a wide range of issues. Although Robertson fared poorly in GOP primaries, the faithful remnant of his campaign has done much better. Supporters have joined together in the Christian Coalition, founded in 1989 by Ralph Reed at Robertson's urging. The Christian Coalition built upon the 1988 Robertson campaign, and steadily gained influence within the GOP, especially after 1990. In the 1992 presidential elections, the Christian Coalition backed George Bush despite a weak attachment among its grassroots members to the sitting president. Partly as a result, Bush's vote total among self-proclaimed religious conservatives was remarkably high. In the 1994 congressional elections the Christian Coalition took much of the credit for reversing party control of the House.

The Christian Coalition leadership has argued that its grassroots members' concerns are broader than the few domestic moral issues historically attributed to it. In 1992 it suppressed the more populist "America First" elements of a large portion of its membership in supporting President Bush over his primary and November challengers, and in 1994 it supported the House GOP "Contract With America," even though that document was silent on domestic moral issues.

The coalition's pro-GOP stance in the 1994 congressional elections, and the clear power of its grassroots vote in achieving a House GOP majority, may not be permanent. For example, the Christian Coalition leadership's support for rolling back federal spending may not have staying power at the grassroots if such a rollback does not appear to produce better economic conditions.

While religious rightists urge others to protect their religious freedoms, their distinction between "the things of this world and the things above" has usually discouraged their own participation. Conservative religious support for the constitutional separation of church and state remains strong despite frequent attacks on present federal court interpretations of the establishment and free-exercise clauses. And in education, many religious traditionalists do not desire direct government support of church-based schools, arguing that the increased influence the church might gain would be more than offset by the moral compromises the church and its leaders would make to maintain such support. They are usually willing to forgo the short-term advantages of support for the longer-term advantages of liberty.

A fourth characteristic of religious traditionalists is their assertion that there must be public signs of private religious conviction. "Religious conservatism" can take two different forms—mental assent to traditional theological concepts or physical obedience to a clear set of rules for daily life. The first is a traditionalism of faith; the second a conservatism of praxis. The conservatism threatened by the Warren Court and the Great Society was the conservatism of praxis. The assertions of conservative praxis—that people can be appropriately guided and adequately cared for by family, neighbor, church, and community, and that political controls in this area are unnecessary and often destructive—were challenged by adventurous Great Society programs and overreaching Supreme Court decisions. These programs and decisions sought to impose—in the view of many religious traditionalists—diversity, pluralism, and relativity of belief that threatened their deepest values and practices.

These characteristics of religious traditionalists—a defensive mentality toward modern American culture, narrow policy goals at the grassroots level, reluctant political involvement, and an emphasis on behavior—usually combine to induce a peculiar form of political action that is well-intentioned but politically naive. Such naivete can be exploited by more seasoned political figures. Groups such as the religious right can become dominated by organizations or individuals with more brazen political motives. At the candidate level, clever political candidates can appeal to the religious conservative's sense of alienation about government domestic policy without fully committing to the religious point of view.

In Congress, Moralist representatives who are friends of the religious right have tremendous freedom of action. They would be very likely to see themselves as trustees, voting in the best moral interests of their constituencies and their own firmly held conservative religious beliefs. The grassroots wants limited government but expanded religious and other traditional authority, so legislative activism is not a highly regarded trait. Especially in a Democratic Congress, Moralists did not need to be active or effective legislators. As such, while Moralist members would see themselves as trustees pursuing the right, they would have a low level of legislative activity characteristic of delegates. These members must support constitutional amendments allowing school prayer or banning abortion, and will almost always oppose attempts to establish hiring preferences for special groups of citizens such as minorities, women, and homosexuals. They also are generally expected to vote against additional domestic spending to reflect a deep-seated belief that lack of morals, not of money, is the fundamental domestic crisis. But Moralist members are in the House primarily to rein in, not expand, Congress's reach.

The New Right

The New Right has deeper Republican roots, more political sophistication, and wider policy goals than the religious right. The New Right's chronic weakness has been a lack of broad grassroots support. In the Reagan-Bush era, the conservative churches presented such a base, but the religious right's fit with the New Right's populist and alienated "Middle-American Radical" stereotypical supporter is at times uncomfortable.[12]

The New Right's alienation is deeper than that of the religious right because the former has a longer list of grievances. New Rightists object to affirmative action, gun control, "coddling" criminals, expensive government programs, and high tax rates that provide few benefits. They dislike foreign imports, foreign property ownership, and communist "appeasement" signaled by low defense spending or high levels of humanitarian or multinational foreign aid.

Much of the New Right is skeptical of wealth, especially older and privileged wealth. New Rightists find little reason to accept or respect this unjust *status quo* of inherited money or power.[13] The New Right's appeal to the lower economic classes contains a significant difficulty. Typically, political alienation encourages political withdrawal. For New Rightists this poses a great problem, which less-alienated religious conservatives help to counteract. As such, the electoral clout of the New Right is concentrated in the religious element because the latter more faithfully participates in at least the basic political process of voting.

New Right elites have long tried to motivate and organize the alienated.[14] Many of the current well-known New Right leaders took part in conservative or Republican politics before the Reagan-Bush era. Richard Viguerie worked for Young Americans for Freedom in the early 1960s; Howard Phillips worked for the Republican National Committee and President Nixon; Paul Weyrich was a Republican Senate aide; Phyllis Schlafly had circulated political writings long before the 1964 Goldwater campaign.[15]

In the late 1970s and early 1980s the religious right became the main target of the New Right's aggressive strategy to fill its grassroots vacuum. New Right organizations were self-identified by the early 1970s, but it was only in 1979 that the decision was made by New Right leaders to try to incorporate the religious right within the New Right network of organizations.[16]

The longer history of the New Right explains its broader political agenda and greater number of active groups. Among the political organizations with which the New Right has direct connections are the American Legislative Exchange Counsel (ALEC), the Heritage Foundation, Young Americans for Freedom (YAF), the National Conservative Political Action Committee (NCPAC), the Committee for the Survival of a Free Congress, and the House Republican Study Committee.

These aspects of the New Right display its differences from the Old Right and religious traditionalists. The Old Right habitually emphasizes New Deal-era disputes such as government waste and anticommunism, essentially arguing with its opponents on various items on the opponents' current national agenda. The New Right is more populist and *ad hoc*, attacking elitism in general and attempting to add new items to the national agenda. For example, it has agitated over issues like the Panama Canal, SDI, and abortion. The methods of the Old Right "regulars" find greater support among longstanding pragmatic and moderate Republicans; the New Right's "realigner" methods recruit new members into politics and in the process alienate some older groups uncomfortable with new issues.

In its association with members of Congress, the New Right has operated chiefly as a GOP intraparty advocacy network. New Right elites provide campaign funding, strategic advice, policy ideas and justifications, staff training and support, honoraria, personal favors, and other benefits to a defined subgroup of Republican members of Congress. The New Right organizations in Washington, D.C., groom, educate, socialize, and patronize these members, seeking to expand the elected representative's social moralism into a broader political view of lower federal taxes, smaller federal government, and more military spending. The American Legislative Exchange Council seeks to bring conservative populist ideas brewing in state legislatures to the attention of lawmakers in Washington, D.C. The Heritage Foundation conducts a wide range of activities from independent issue research to media efforts to coalition building and information exchange among conservative interest groups. Its publications flood the Washington offices of Republican lawmakers. Young Americans For Freedom and other conservative groups like the Leadership Institute recruit and train young persons in conservative ideas and political action. Free Congress, directly or through other groups that its leader Paul Weyrich started or helped form, is heavily involved in fundraising, grassroots agitation, and more recently electronic media with NET, National Empowerment Television.

Much of this activity successfully socializes new House Republicans. New Right members of Congress vote predictably, scoring at the extreme right pole of most voting scales. A particular brand of member is developed by these New Right associations, active in national politics and issues but not necessarily active in the legislative process of a Democratic Congress.

New Right behavior would clearly be like that of the trustee model, with an interest in the Washington, D.C., community overshadowing constituency outreach efforts. Indeed, many representatives under the influence of the New Right are labeled by the media as "activists," but they are not *legislative* activists. Alienated from the traditional national government paradigm, New Rightists seldom participate in the dealmaking and compromise prevalent in legislative politics. Rather, they confine their legislative activity to broad initiatives to cut taxes or limit government's regulatory or spending power that will face no serious consideration in a Democratic Congress. In a Democratic House, their activity was channeled outside the traditional legislative process, especially in electoral and strategic politics, seeking to develop and "test market" elite New Right ideas with receptive grassroots constituencies.

In the Reagan-Bush era, the New Right and religious right operated mostly as distinct but complementary movements. In the early and middle portions of the era, religious conservatives broadened the grassroots base of New Right elites. At the end of the era, the religious movement became more organized at the elite level to alter the focus of traditional New Right elite organizations.

At first New Right elites led the way, giving selected politicians financial and intellectual resources for them to pursue their individual goals. This relationship grew with Congress's institutional and campaign reforms of the 1970s. The New Right's attempt in the late 1970s to merge its elite organs with the popular strength of the religious right was as much a strategic choice as a natural fit. But the attempt to capture the religious grassroots to pursue broader New Right aims has not turned out quite as the New Right envisioned. Rather than capturing the grassroots, those grassroots have developed a set of its own elites, chiefly the Christian Coalition, that has captured many New Right organizations.

Although there are tensions between the New Right and religious right, there is a mostly common ideology joining the two groups that is unlikely to sever them.[17] The strong working relationship between these two groups obscures those few religiously conservative House Republican members outside the New Right movement. For example, while they served in the House both Republican Protestant Paul Henry of Michigan and GOP Catholic Tom Tauke of Iowa openly identified themselves as conservative evangelical Christians. Their votes on moral issues like abortion and obscenity were solidly in line with the grassroots religious right. But they often deviated from the broader New Right agenda on foreign policy, social spending, labor, and environmental issues. Neither man was fully welcomed by New Right elites.

On the other side of the coin, not all New Right activists practice what the religious right preaches. The tragedies of NCPAC's Terry Dolan and former GOP Representatives Bob Bauman and Buz Lukens,[18] all New Right figures, embarrassed the religious elements of the New Right coalition.

More important for this analysis, these anecdotes illustrate the periodic tension in the early and middle portions of the Reagan-Bush era between the fervor of the religious grassroots and the calculation of New Right elites. Although conflicts occurred, they were the exceptions. In general, GOP lawmakers elected by religiously motivated citizens either accepted the broader New Right agenda as candidates, or adopted it upon election. In the latter portion of the Reagan-Bush era and beyond, religious conservatives held the upper hand. Republican elites had to court them, and urge them to broaden their religious agenda in the interest of electoral success.

Nowhere was this pattern clearer than in the development of the House Republican "Contract with America" for the 1994 campaign. The Christian Coalition leadership agreed to the contract's silence on traditional moral issues such as school prayer, abortion, and homosexuality in order to focus the contract on economic issues and attract independents, especially 1992 Perot voters who are agnostic on many socially conservative issues. New religious elites cannot allow the GOP to remain silent if these elites hope to maintain the current level of grassroots support.

Neoconservatism

Neoconservatism is that portion of American political thought and action that split from the Democratic party during the Vietnam War era. Neoconservatism began as a distinct intellectual movement in the middle 1960s, and achieved visibility in the early 1970s. Many neoconservative leaders were once active supporters of the New Deal, and even socialists. They broke with the Democrats over what they saw as the excesses of the 1960s policies.[19] Neoconservatives also criticized what they called the "New Class" of social engineers who tried to fine tune the economy, social behavior, and the international order beyond reasonable expectations.[20]

The movement grew so fast in part because of the intellectual, political, and media sophistication of its adherents. Neoconservatism is an intellectual movement, and neoconservatives are especially comfortable in the Washington, D.C., policy advocacy, political journal, and think tank environment. *Public Interest, This World,* and *Commentary* are the most prominent neoconservative journals, with a limited but elite readership.

Neoconservatives bring methodological and quantitative proficiency, which is useful in much contemporary political debate. Gottfried and Fleming noted that neoconservatives "revel in statistics and computerized information,"[21] even though they are sometimes criticized for their managerial and "social engineering" approach.[22] Adherents believe that social problems are amenable to rigorous investigation that can point to carefully calculated adjustments to public policy.

Neoconservatives can support a welfare state that is "properly managed." Indeed, the neoconservative state model is a mixed economy and a bureaucratically managed democracy. The representative's proper task is to prune government's overgrowth and to rationalize its actions, not to destroy its essentially sound premise.

Neoconservatives acknowledge that social values change over time and, like positional conservatives and not ideological conservatives, they embrace traditional values more to slow this change than to reverse it.[23] This approach contrasts with both the religious perspective that sees social ills as a consequence of weak personal ethics, and with the libertarian view that personal behavior is not a government concern. This faith in the possibilities of intelligent government is an aspect of neoconservative ideology that ties them to older Republicans and distinguishes them from other more recent members of the Republican coalition.

Neoconservatives stand apart from older GOP conservative groups as well, chiefly in their activist foreign policy. The former envision an American-led global democratic order that includes military means to advance democracy around the world. While less conservative Republicans would oppose defense spending and other military engagements, most neoconservatives believe that the United States has an obligation to proselytize the world for American values.

Neoconservatives portray themselves as political centrists. Indeed, the combination of a middling domestic policy and activist pro-interventionist foreign policy puts them near the center of unidimensional measures. In addition, it potentially allows them to return to the Democratic fold under the right circumstances, as some did in 1992.

During most of the Reagan-Bush era, neoconservatives aligned themselves with the GOP and gave many of the party's traditional conservative principles greater intellectual grounding. Neoconservatives also directed funds, staff, and intellectual energy to leading established conservative think tanks such as the Hoover Institution, the Heritage Foundation, and the American Enterprise Institute.[24]

The neoconservative impact on congressional Republicans is similar to that of the New Right, and efforts between the two groups are often coordinated. Indeed, in the early 1990s it became increasingly difficult to distinguish the New Right from neoconservatives, as the former became more established in the Washington, D.C., policy environment and the latter became more comfortably Republican. As such, by 1995 leading neoconservatives such as Irving Kristol were acknowledging that it was now difficult to make a clear distinction between neoconservatism and politically active conservative strains of thought other than libertarianism.[25]

Post-reform GOP lawmakers influenced by neoconservatives would illustrate trustee behavior—a lot of Washington, D.C., activity, but much of it outside the lawmaking process. For these members, neoconservatives provide policy ideas and justifications, and educate them in neoconservative ideas. Particularly in foreign and defense policy before the end of the Cold War, neoconservative objectives were similar to the New Right and there was significant cooperation. On moral issues, however, the former prefer to emphasize the pragmatic reasons for promoting traditional family values; the New Right argument is more populist, dogmatic, and antigovernment.

In some constitutional, economic, and budget policies the neoconservatives differ greatly from the New Right. The former are more interested in preserving church-state separation. Key neoconservative thinkers are Jewish or Catholic, groups historically threatened by militant Protestantism and New Right populism.[26] As the post-reform era wore on and House partisanship grew, however, the two emphases became more complementary as each worked with the House GOP in devising legislative alternatives.

Neoconservatives are, however, more interested than the New Right in improving domestic policy, a characteristic that often serves as an advantage in the legislative process. Because constituency expectations require members of Congress to attend to domestic matters, neoconservative domestic policy analysis is used by many House Republicans, especially those in the Moderate faction. Creating new policy alternatives, rather than merely criticizing the old and urging their repeal, is especially helpful to Republican members of Congress seeking domestic policy credentials to counter criticism of their votes against most current domestic programs. Lawmakers attracted to neoconservatives include those traditionally active in the legislative process and those interested in putting new issues on the legislative agenda. These lawmakers would be quite active legislatively and in issue-oriented caucuses on Capitol Hill.

Libertarianism

Libertarianism is the purest ideological element in the new GOP, but the one with the least focused organization. Rather than establishing a separate identity, libertarian-leaning representatives have influenced the thinking of more organized New Right and neoconservative leaders. The libertarian opposes government involvement in economic and personal matters and is cautious about aggressive foreign policies. Economics is the most important policy area for libertarians; they have warmed to supply-side economics mostly because it stressed fiscal questions about the size and scope of government. Libertarians are, however, quite uncomfortable with the moralism of the religious right/New Right coalition, and they are disturbed by neoconservative internationalism. Because domestic economic issues tend to draw libertarians to the GOP while social policy pushes them away, libertarian Republicans are subject to intense intraparty cross pressures. At the same time, their intellectual defense of liberty against government has appealed to the intellectualism of the neoconservatives and the alienation of the New and religious rights.

Libertarianism has been more an intellectual than popular movement since its ancestor, classical liberalism, was first articulated by John Locke. William Maddox and Stuart Lillie identified six tenets of classical liberalism to which American libertarians subscribe in a modified form today: individualism, an instrumental view of the state, limited government, individual rights, legal equality, and representative government.[27] These six tenets cluster around two domestic policy questions—the proper role of government and the prescriptions for apparent social inequalities.

Libertarian social thought nicely buttresses traditional Republican ideas of limited government and the new supply-side economics popularized by President Reagan. The supply-side argument for stimulative tax cuts imposes additional limits on the size of government, an end desirable to libertarians. But other elements of supply-side economics make it less attractive to libertarians. Some supply-siders influenced by neoconservative thinking emphasize the revenue-generating aspects of stimulative tax cuts more than the shrinking of the government's reach. Libertarians suspect that these supply-siders are little concerned, ultimately, about the size of government.

Libertarian evaluations of recent Republican foreign and social policy are also complex. While libertarians appreciate growing world commerce, they are skeptical of government claims on private resources to build large militaries and to provide foreign aid. Libertarians would also tend to disagree with other Republicans on immigration, focusing on the potential economic benefits of a larger workforce and worrying less about preserving a unique American culture.

The remainder of the new Republican domestic agenda is also problematic for libertarians. Libertarians may agree with GOP moves to restrain affirmative action. While they support the rights of individuals of any race to share in the economic system, libertarians do not think that massive government intervention would be required to achieve that goal. Libertarians join easily with other Republicans to support color-blind "equal opportunity."

The rise of "family" issues in the national Republican party makes libertarians very uncomfortable. Individual rights for the libertarian extend to matters of personal behavior. Interference in lifestyles must be resisted as firmly as interference in the market. Libertarians reject extreme regulation of drugs and alcohol; state protection or promotion of prayer or other aspects of organized religion; and restrictions on abortion, homosexuality, and other "immoral" private activities.

The voting record of Republicans holding tightly to libertarianism would differ sharply from most others. The libertarian opposition to military assertiveness links them to the few remaining liberal Republicans and to a persistent but small vein of Republican isolationism. Libertarian Republicans would be more conservative on economic issues than on social or foreign policy as these issues are usually measured by interest groups. Libertarian distaste for government would indicate low traditional legislative activity such as bill sponsorship or cosponsorship for libertarian-leaning lawmakers. Libertarian members might be seen as fairly inactive, isolationists who vote moderately on social and foreign policy issues but conservatively on economic matters. As such, their behavior on the trustee-delegate dimension would indicate, looking at the Washington, D.C., data used in this analysis, that they could be categorized as delegates. A more accurate assessment might be, however, that these members come from low-demand districts that are easily won by inactive conservative legislators. While there are few House Republicans who fit this description well, one former House Republican, Ron Paul of Texas, later ran for president on the Libertarian Party ticket.

The individualism of libertarian thought would, almost by definition, tend to discourage elite organization. In fact, libertarian think tanks and interest groups are few; the only prominent Washington-based groups are the increasingly influential Cato Institute and the smaller Competitive Enterprise Institute. Cato has especially grown in influence with the reassertion of domestic economic issues, the area most comfortable with Republican philosophy, at the center of House Republican policy.

The Old Right

Many House Republicans in the Reagan-Bush era operated from a position still rooted in reaction against the New Deal/Great Society platform. This old frame of reference can perhaps be best characterized by its critics in various new conservative movements. Neoconservative Irving Kristol wrote, for example, that Old Right Republicans are the kind that Democrats considered "appropriate":

It has long been a cliche of liberal discourse that what this country needs is a truly intelligent and sophisticated conservatism. . . . This . . . . desirable conservatism should have a philosophic and literary dimension which would rectify the occasional excesses of liberal ideology. It should even have a nebulous but definitely genteel political dimension, since it is likely that we shall always, at interval, need a brief interregnum of conservative government whose function it is to consolidate and ratify liberal reforms.[28]

In the dominant New Deal paradigm that Kristol attacked, the ideal Republican is a "cultured" Eisenhower; pleasant but unimaginative. Kristol's implication was that traditional conservatism is positionally conservative, opposed to the New Deal set of issues but neither intellectually nor politically vigorous enough to propose a different agenda.

Another summation of traditional Republican conservatism is found in a 1960 essay "Why I Am Not A Conservative," by libertarian Friedrich Hayek.[29]

> Let me now state what seems to me the decisive objection to . . . conservatism. It is that by its very nature it cannot offer an alternative to the direction in which we are moving. It may succeed by its resistance to current tendencies in slowing down undesirable developments, but, since it does not indicate another direction, it cannot prevent their continuance. It has, for this reason, invariably been the fate of conservatism to be dragged along a path not of its own choosing.[30]

One of positional conservatism's fundamental traits is its fear of change, even when it is nominally in charge of a government. For Hayek, this fear leads to passivity. It also leads conservatives, when they obtain political power, to use it merely to slow change or freeze at the *status quo*. From Hayek's libertarian perspective, Old Guard conservatives fall into the two errors of fondness for government authority and insufficient appreciation of market forces.[31] In the American context, the resulting policies only consolidate the New Deal/ Great Society agenda, reestablishing its credibility to allow it to advance further once Democrats regain control.

The attacks on Old Guard Republican conservatism by neoconservative Kristol and classical liberal Hayek find support in recent American political events. Republican presidents and representatives from World War II through the late 1970s can hardly be accused of generating a surplus of creative ideas. The Eisenhower and Nixon presidencies were essentially consolidations, and in some cases expansions, of Democratic domestic policies. Republican lawmakers did not fundamentally challenge congressional norms or propose vastly different policies.

Republicanism did not revive in a policy sense until the mid-1970s when religious traditionalism, New Right populism, libertarian individualism in economic policy, and neoconservative intellectualism in foreign and social policy enabled the GOP to respond more directly to Democrats. In many ways, the Republican Party revived in spite of, not because of, Old Guard leaders.

The behavioral characteristics of the Old Guard would vary. In terms of the delegate-trustee distinction, activism for Old Guard members would depend on tenure. Junior members would have low legislative activity levels, a characteristic of delegates. As they followed the traditional apprenticeship norm, in time they would be given greater legislative responsibilities by the leadership. Consequently, only after several terms would legislative activity rise.

Hayek's decades-old critique of conservatism has remarkable parallels to many of the charges made against Old Guard conservative Republicans in the 1989 Gingrich-Madigan Whip race. The Old Guard was accused of being too pragmatic, passive and even secretly in league with the Democratic majority. Such charges resonated with the younger and more activist elements of the broad-based coalition that supported Gingrich.

Each conservative element had followers in the House Republican conferences of the post-reform era, and the proportion of influence changed greatly during that period. Overall, the neoconservative movement has the most significant intellectual weight, for it brings rational justification for an aggressive foreign policy and a reasoned domestic policy critique inoculated against accusations of social insensitivity. Religious traditionalists provide most of the foot soldiers and some of the popular outrage necessary to challenge the secularization of American politics. The New Right elite offered organizational skills to the religious conservatives and expanded the movement to a broader populist coalition now directed mostly by religious activists. Libertarianism is fertile soil for antigovernment sentiment that unites the disparate elements of the party on economic policy. Its clear ideological expression gives additional ammunition to the other ideological groups trying to shoot down big government.

There are internal disagreements in the party over foreign, social, and economic policy sometimes masked by votes. All new conservative factions united, with the Old Guard, against the set of federal domestic spending programs promoted by congressional Democrats in the post-reform era. Neoconservatives argued against them because of their poor performance; religious conservatives opposed them because they undermined moral rectitude; the New Right agitated against them because they were "big government"; the old Right voted against them since that is what they always did. Libertarian thought gave each group additional reasons for their position.

The domestic social agenda creates more easily observed divisions. Most of the New Right and religious conservatives support traditional lifestyles. Neoconservatives are sympathetic to the society envisioned by their coalition members, but they object to coercive measures given their greater culture diversity. Old Rightists join here with the neoconservatives, as the former are uncomfortable with the new "moralization" of politics. Members influenced by Libertarian thought object strongly to the social agenda as outside appropriate political discussion, seeking to put off discussion of its elements or defer those decisions to states or federal courts.

On foreign and defense policy, most groups are united with varied levels of enthusiasm for "pax Americana" or an American-led New World Order. These ideas are pushed most strongly by neoconservatives and New Rightists, and opposed most strongly by libertarians. The Old Guard and many religious conservatives are often in the middle, sharing at least some of the isolationist preference of the libertarians.

Summary

The infusion of new ideologies and concerns has made the GOP far more diverse than usually described. In Reiter's terminology, two "Realigner" groups have infiltrated the party. This infiltration has occurred at several levels, especially in some local and state party organizations, and including Congress. First, a New Right coalition embraces alienated elites, populists, and religionists. The religionists are now dominant in a growing "Moralist" faction in Congress. Second, a neoconservative network holds together "Enterprisers" focused on economic growth and legislative creativity. That group appeals to Republicans of nearly all stripes who are searching for positive alternatives to the traditional Democratic framework and agenda. Libertarians have given greater credence to some elements of supply-side economics and greater energy to attempts to roll back the "welfare state," mostly abetting the energy of the New Right and the thinking of neoconservatives.

Republican congressional politics is more complex because of these new elements. Positional conservatives are joined in the Conference by ideological conservatives from several groups. In its opposition mode during most of the period examined here, this complexity provided more reasons for the minority congressional party to oppose the majority in votes, other behaviors and general attitudes. Members in these factions joined against majority legislation, but they often quarreled about internal party matters or congressional norms. The result of these new influences is a complex party membership divided by several ideologies, views of the institution of Congress, and the proper role of lawmakers.

Modeling Intraparty Divisions

The complexity of this new environment provided more reasons in the post-reform era for the minority congressional party to oppose the majority in votes on the House floor, making the minority appear united. At the same time, the new elements caused greater House Republican divergence along behavioral and attitudinal lines, creating a wide range of factions not defined strictly by voting differences. Members attached to any faction might unite with others to oppose legislation, but they often splintered and quarreled when dealing with internal party matters or congressional norms.

The challenge is to identify data that make reasonable distinctions among these factions, explaining voting behavior as well as other important activities such as leadership selection. This analysis, as do other studies, uses voting data as a critical source of information. *National Journal* economic, social, and foreign policy scores, and National Taxpayers Union spending scores are the voting-based data used in this study. *National Journal* scores are also used to derive a fiscal conservatism score in an attempt to identify different patterns of voting activity.

A wide range of behavioral data are also used. Floor and other legislative activity, standing committee, party committee, and caucus data are all employed to quantify different types and levels of member interest and behavior.

Information is gathered for all Republican members of the U.S. House of Representatives who served at least one full term between 1980 and 1994. Voting data are calculated for each Congress, not for each member across all the Congresses in which he or she served. Activity data are, however, calculated in the aggregate, with each member having only one, constant, legislative activity and national activity score across all the Congresses.

The justification for this disparate treatment is simple. Because of congressional turnover and the seniority norm, committee preferences for incoming members, especially those desiring influence committees, are not usually met until the second or later terms. In addition, caucus selection comes late in the decision-making cycle of new members, and is probably not completely formed until a member's second or third term. Legislative activity is also muted in one's first term. Thus, for these activity measures it seems more accurate to compile one average score for each member.

In total, more than 300 House Republicans are analyzed in this study and placed into factions. As implied by the discussion of the various ideological movements in the Republican party, labeling these factions is a somewhat artificial exercise. One commentator identified "yuppies and evangelicals" as two new elements of the GOP presidential coalition with followers in Congress.[32] Presumably, yuppies find some appeal in neoconservative intellectualism, libertarian amoralism, and supply-side economics; and evangelicals support the conservative domestic social agenda. A Times Mirror scheme has identified "Enterprisers" and "Moralists" as key parts of GOP electoral victories in the Reagan-Bush era, terms that are more descriptive of the agenda and interests of these factions in the House GOP. This study employs some of the labels used by A. James Reichley, others used in the Times Mirror analysis, and proposes a few novel labels in finding seven House Republican factions.

These factions are Enterprisers, Moralists, Moderates, Patricians, Stalwarts, Provincials, and Placeholders. The first two groups are relatively new and tied, respectively, to neoconservatism and the New Right/religious right. The third and fourth groups are of longer standing in the party and quite active in the legislative process, but were and remain outside the GOP mainstream. Moderates are policy oriented members with long traditions as "pragmatists" willing to work with a Democratic House majority on selected issues. Many have neoconservative connections, which grew stronger after the heightened partisanship of the post-reform era shut them out of congressional activity. Patricians are also policy oriented, and come from the liberal, progressive wing of the GOP usually thought to be dying out.

The last three groups form the traditional core of the House GOP, with Stalwarts the bedrock of House Republican positional conservatism. Provincials and Placeholders, the former overall quite conservative and the latter quite moderate, were involved very little in the partisan and procedural controversies of the post-reform era. They seemed to operate quite comfortably in the old New Deal/Great Society paradigm, with individual members of each faction able to work quietly and constructively with Democratic party members to obtain narrow benefits for local constituencies.

Decisions over the order and priority of distinctions are discussed as each faction is examined. Some of these decisions are clear and easily made, while others are less obvious and more difficult. Disagreements over the precise points on *National Journal* scales that distinguish among conservatism, moderation, and liberalism, for example, are open to continuous dispute. In general, the most influential information used in distinguishing factions are the *National Journal* scores, and the fiscal conservative ratio developed from those scores. The various activity measures also figure strongly into the analysis.

There is no fixed mathematical formula or statistical straitjacket into which the data are forced and by which members are assigned to factions. The approach of this analysis is less rigid. The intent is not to achieve perfect results. Rather, the approach seeks to describe factions based on a fuller understanding of the ideological complexity and strategic disagreement within the party during the post-reform Congress and now in the new situation of a Republican House.

Notes

1. Roger Davidson, *The Role of the Congressman* (New York: Pegasus, 1969), 117.

2. A. James Reichley, *Conservatives in an Age of Change: The Nixon and Ford Administrations* (Washington, D.C.: Brookings Institution, 1981), 6–11 passim.

3. Samuel Lubell's notion of a "sun" and "moon" in political parties, with the majority defining the political cosmos and the minority forced to reflect that "light" is applicable here. The point for House Republicans is that more ideological members refused to operate as the "moon" for the Democratic "sun."

4. Michael Malbin, "Factions and Incentives in Congress," *Public Interest* 86 (Winter 1987) 91–108.

5. John S. Saloma III, "Old Right? New Right? *One* Right," *The Nation*, 14 January 1984, 14–18.

6. Andrew Heywood, *Political Ideologies: An Introduction* (New York: St Martin's Press, 1992).

7. Paul Gottfried and Thomas Fleming, *The Conservative Movement* (Boston: Twayne Publishers, 1988), 96–111 passim.

8. Problematic but widely cited analyses include Saloma, 14–18, and John Lukacs, "The American Conservatives: Where They Came From and Where They are Going," *Harpers*, January 1984, 44–49.

9. Each of these groups are distinct, but frequently misunderstood, elements of conservative Christianity. For example, evangelicals compose a broad category of Christians from various denominations and independent churches, chiefly distinguished by an emphasis on personal religious conversion. Fundamentalists, on the other hand, are a smaller group distinguished by a literalist interpretation of the Bible. While there is some overlap in these groups, there are also many tensions. For an excellent breakdown of politically conservative elements along denominational lines see, for example, Corwin

Smidt, "Evangelicals within Contemporary American Politics: Differentiating between Fundamentalist and Non-Fundamentalist Evangelicals," *Western Political Quarterly* 41 (September 1988): 601–20.

10. Tim LaHaye, *The Battle for the Mind*, cited in Sara Diamond, *Spiritual Warfare: The Politics of the Christian Right* (Boston: South End Press, 1989), 85.

11. The domestic categories of populist and conservative are two of four identified by William S. Maddox and Stuart A. Lillie, *Beyond Liberal and Conservative: Reassessing the Political Spectrum* (Washington, D.C.: Cato Institute, 1984).

12. Donald I. Warren, *The Radical Center: Middle Americans and the Politics of Alienation* (South Bend: University of Notre Dame Press, 1976).

13. Linda J. Medcalf and Kenneth M. Dolbeare, *Neopolitics: American Political Ideas in the 1980s* (Philadelphia: Temple University Press, 1985), 166.

14. Gottfried, 77.

15. Gottfried, 78.

16. Medcalf, 169.

17. Gottfried, 90.

18. Dolan was apparently homosexual and died of AIDS; Bauman was caught by Capitol police in an act of sodomy; Lukens was convicted of having sex with a female minor.

19. Medcalf, 133.

20. Medcalf, 133.

21. Gottfried, 65.

22. See, for example, George Gilder, "Why I Am Not A Neoconservative," *National Review*, 5 March 1982, 218–22.

23. David L. Bender, *The Political Spectrum*, 2d ed. (St. Paul, Minn.: Greenhaven Press, 1986), 193.

24. Gottfried, 73.

25. Irving Kristol, "American Conservatism 1945–1995," *Public Interest* 94 (Fall 1995): 80–91.

26. Isodore Silver, "Neoconservatism vs. Conservatism?" *Commonweal*, 31 July 1981, 430.

27. Maddox, 9–12 passim.

28. Irving Kristol, "Confessions of a True, Self-Confessed—Perhaps the Only—Neoconservative," *Public Opinion* 2 (1979): 50–52.

29. Friedrich Hayek, "Why I Am Not A Conservative" in Donald Bender, *The Political Spectrum*, 2d ed. (St. Paul, Minn.: Greenhaven Press, 1986), 151–59.

30. Hayek, 152.

31. Hayek, 154.

32. Ronald Brownstein, "Yuppies and Evangelicals: The Shaky GOP Coalition," *Nation*, 15 March 1986, 301.

Chapter 4

Policy-Oriented House Republican Factions

The discussion of House Republican factions has two sections, based upon the fundamental division between a member's relatively greater interest in national policy or local constituency matters. The first section of this discussion, which composes most of this chapter, reviews the four policy-oriented factions of Enterprisers, Moralists, Moderates, and Patricians. The second section, chapter five, discusses the three constituency-oriented factions of Stalwarts, Provincials, and Placeholders.

This initial distinction between policy and constituency orientation is justified by examining a number of measures used in this analysis—specifically standing committee memberships by type, the level of party committee memberships, and the level and type of caucus and intraparty group memberships. The distinction among committee types—namely policy, constituency, and influence committees—is adapted from the work of Steven Smith and Christopher Deering.[1] Their list of Appropriations, Budget, Rules, and Ways and Means as "prestige" committees is extended and modified by adding Standards of Official Conduct (Ethics) and Intelligence to a group of "influence" committees. Their list of "policy" committees is duplicated here, and to their list of "constituency" committees is added the House Post Office and Civil Service Committee. The extent and content of policy activities of members is a special interest of this book, and the division of the discussion into policy- and non-policy oriented factions fosters this interest. Two policy-oriented or activist factions—Moralists and Enterprisers—are conservative and have tended to cluster in like-thinking intraparty groups such as the Conservative Opportunity Soci-

89

ety and the Republican Study Committee. Two other factions—Patricians and Moderates—work together in moderate or liberal intra-party groups like the House Wednesday Group and the now-defunct '92 Group.

The three other factions are less interested in legislative activity and national policy and have less ideological voting patterns. They also tend to have lower overall committee and caucus membership levels, and these memberships are preponderantly in constituency-oriented committees and caucuses.

Table 4.1 below illustrates the various committee activities of the seven identified factions, and the overall legislative activity of each faction for the 101st Congress of 1989–90. The House Republican Conference in the 101st Congress of 1989–90 is chosen for illustration, since that group is a typical House Republican Conference of the late Reagan-Bush years, and it was a pivotal period in the House party's strategic history because Newt Gingrich was elected Whip during that Congress. The information on the table, which lists the factions from most conservative to least conservative *National Journal* mean scores, offers several insights. First, the number of influence committee slots is centered in the middle of the party, not at the extremes. The Stalwarts, Provincials, and Moderates have proportionally the greatest number of influence committee slots, and they all cluster at the voting center of the party (the *NJ* mean of the Placeholders is only slightly lower than that of the Moderates). Second, influence committee memberships are almost inversely related to legislative activity, i.e., the

TABLE 4.1
Committee Placements and Legislative Activity of House Republican Factions (101st Congress)

	Policy Committee	Constituency Committee	Influence Committee	Legislative Activity
Moralist	0.39	1.12	0.18	1.03
Enterpriser	0.62	0.71	0.24	1.02
Stalwart	0.67	0.60	0.38	0.87
Provincial	0.44	0.72	0.44	0.86
Placeholder	0.21	0.93	0.29	0.99
Moderate	0.75	0.55	0.40	1.14
Patrician	0.64	0.91	0.18	1.38
Average	0.55	0.79	0.31	1.00

factions with high legislative activity are those with low influence committee memberships. The only exception is Moderates, who are well-represented on influence committees and are also legislatively active. Third, most of the active groups are at the voting extremes of the party. The relative numerical strength of the policy-oriented factions has changed over time. As table 4.2 shows, Moralists and Enterprisers have grown significantly in the Reagan-Bush era, while Moderates have grown modestly and Patricians have nearly died out.

The methodology here allows the same member to be placed in different factions in different congresses, depending upon change in behavior. As a result, some migration among factions may occur. Among policy-oriented factions, many of the Patricians became identified as Moderates as they came to vote slightly more conservatively. These movements are usually rare. In any case, to compensate it seems best to consider the policy-oriented factions in two pairs, the two conservative factions and the two moderate factions.

Arranging the factions in this way reveals a clear policy activism shift in the Reagan-Bush era. While early in the period more moderates than conservatives participated in policy activities, the moderate activists were soon swamped by conservative activists, and by the 103rd Congress of 1993–94 were outnumbered more than three to one.

The study data for the policy-oriented factions are presented in the following series of tables. The first such table, table 4.3, shows the geographic distribution of the policy factions, in terms of the percent of each faction in one of seven regions. The table also compares the factional distribution to that of the entire House GOP. While these regional concentrations will be addressed at length later, this table already shows the regional origins of the two pairs of policy-oriented factions, the conservative policy groups from the South, Plains/Rockies, and Pacific, and the moderate groups from the Mid-Atlantic, Midwest, and New England.

TABLE 4.2
Policy Factions in Each Congress
(Percentage of Conference)

	Congress						
	97th	98th	99th	100th	101st	102nd	103rd
Moralist	7.3	15.0	21.7	14.7	18.9	22.3	21.6
Enterpriser	9.4	21.6	18.9	24.9	19.4	16.3	14.8
Moderate	5.7	9.0	10.6	11.3	11.4	9.0	10.8
Patrician	14.1	6.0	6.7	5.7	6.3	3.0	1.1

TABLE 4.3
Geographic Distribution of Policy Factions
(Percentage of Faction in Region)

	New England	Middle Atlantic	Border States	Mid-West	South	Plains/ Rockies	Pacific
Moralist	0.0	6.1	9.1	12.1	39.4	21.2	12.1
Enterpriser	0.0	5.9	5.9	14.7	26.5	17.6	29.4
Moderate	10.0	40.0	0.0	25.0	5.0	5.0	15.0
Patrician	45.5	46.5	9.1	9.1	0.0	0.0	0.0
Average	5.7	17.1	8.0	22.3	20.0	12.6	14.3

TABLE 4.4
Policy Faction Voting Data Scores

	NJ Economic	NJ Social	NJ Foreign	NJ Mean	Fiscal Conserv.	NTU
Moralist	10.53	4.35	7.38	7.42	1.25	83.95
Enterpriser	9.26	13.12	7.74	10.04	1.90	79.16
Moderate	31.25	44.50	38.35	38.03	1.40	69.80
Patrician	44.77	67.91	58.68	57.45	1.42	53.22
Average	20.33	23.38	20.13	21.28	1.25	73.56

This study also collected data on the voting patterns of all faction members. These results, mean scores for each faction on various *National Journal* measures, are shown in table 4.4. Almost all policy-oriented factions share a high relative fiscal conservatism as identified by the fiscal conservatism ratio measure. The only exception is the Moralists, whose extremely low *NJ* social policy scores keep their fiscal conservatism ratio relatively small.

Several types of behavioral activities were also collected for each member of Congress. Committee memberships, legislative and other activity levels, and caucus membership commitments were tabulated for each member. The following three tables illustrate that data. Table 4.5 lists the standing committee memberships for activist factions; table 4.6 the activity levels for these same factions, and table 4.7 their caucus memberships.

The analysis describes each faction in general terms, identifying its distinguishing characteristics, geographical distribution, and some of its most prominent or representative members. Included is commentary on the faction's relative size and strength throughout the post-reform era. The analytical presentation consists largely of comparing

TABLE 4.5
Policy Faction Standing Committee Memberships

		Committee Type	
	Policy	**Constituency**	**Influence**
Moralist	0.39	1.21	0.18
Enterpriser	0.62	0.71	0.24
Moderate	0.75	0.55	0.40
Patrician	0.64	0.91	0.18
Average	0.55	0.79	0.31

TABLE 4.6
Policy Faction Activity Levels

	Party Committees	**Legislative Activity**	**National Activity**
Moralist	1.35	1.03	3.64
Enterpriser	3.06	1.02	6.82
Moderate	2.05	1.14	7.20
Patrician	2.00	1.38	7.55
Average	1.97	1.00	5.23

TABLE 4.7
Policy Faction Caucus Memberships

	Intraparty	**National**	**Local**	**Total**
Moralist	0.79	0.91	1.58	3.27
Enterpriser	0.94	1.97	1.35	4.26
Moderate	1.25	2.75	1.60	5.60
Patrician	1.45	3.27	1.91	6.64
Average	0.85	1.58	1.42	3.85

scores on the data that have been collected and the measures that have been developed, as presented in the above tables.

Conservative Policy-Oriented Factions: Enterprisers and Moralists

Enterprisers and Moralists are the two most prominent factions in the present House Republican party. In fact, the six top elected House

Republican leadership positions in the 104th Congress are all held by members identified as Moralists and Enterprisers.

Despite their monopoly in the leadership, these two factions are relatively recent additions to the House GOP coalition. These two groups grew from a combined 16 percent of the House GOP Conference in the 97th Congress of 1981–82 (14 Moralists and 18 Enterprisers in a Conference of 192 members), to 36 percent in the 103rd Congress of 1993–94 (38 Moralists and 26 Enterprisers out of a Conference with 176 members).

The names of each faction deliberately imply several attitudes of members in those factions. "Enterpriser" implies the image of a business proponent, who is sympathetic to business interests and who has conservative but not rigidly narrow social attitudes. These aspects of the definition reveal the Enterprisers' belief in market forces over government. They also reflect a far deeper interest by Enterprisers in deregulating the economy than in regulating personal social behavior, although faction members do tend to vote quite conservatively on social issues. While they would generally support social conservatives, that is not where their personal interests or activities concentrate.

The term also suggests traits of activity, ambition, innovation, and optimism. One could expect Enterprisers to be active in all aspects of congressional activity including standing committees, party committees, and caucuses. All these dimensions of the term can be applied to the behaviors, outlooks, and ambitions of House GOP Enterprisers.

The term Moralist brings to mind a person focused on issues of personal conduct. Moralists may believe in a growing market and a shrinking federal budget. At the same time, the term implies a willingness, greater than that of Enterprisers, to regulate the personal behavior of individuals. In the political arena, the term also implies a focus on the conduct of oneself and one's colleagues, as well as personal behavior in society generally, rather than on traditional public policy issues. Thus, Moralists might try to broaden the public agenda beyond budget and fiscal issues to issues of social behavior. At the same time, they might not be very active in the political process, despite their interest in policy, because they evaluate others and choose to be evaluated themselves by their personal moral conduct and not their type of substantive representational activity. They prefer to be known as moral persons rather than as effective legislators. Finally, the term Moralist implies a judgmental attitude toward others. Again, these different shades of meaning are intended.

Moralists and Enterprisers have similar voting profiles, similar negative attitudes to the congressional norms of the Democratic post-reform era, and similar representational styles. Moralists were more hostile to the moral relativism they saw in the Democrats' defense of individual rights, fearing excessive permissiveness. Enterprisers were more hostile to the policy outcomes of a partisan Democratic Congress. Both factions were hostile to the Washington policy climate of the 1980s and early 1990s, and joined in an attempt to overthrow it.

The similarity of concerns, especially toward the institution, are illustrated in the Gingrich-Madigan Whip vote in the 101st Congress, as 61 percent of Enterprisers and 66 percent of Moralists supported Enterpriser Gingrich. Gingrich received about 50 percent of his total support from these two groups even though at the time they composed about one-third of House Republicans. No other factions gave Gingrich greater shares of support.

Enterprisers

Table 4.2 lists the percentage of Enterprisers in each Republican Conference from 1981 through 1994. As these data show, the size of the Enterpriser faction jumped after the 1982 mid-term election. Despite the loss of twenty-five House GOP seats, Enterprisers had twice as many members in the 98th Congress of 1983–84 as in the 97th Congress, doubling from eighteen to thirty-six. Enterpriser numbers remained high and stable throughout most of the Reagan-Bush era, despite a small decline in the faction's relative power in the early 1990s.

The regional distribution of the Enterpriser faction (table 4.3) is also important. In the 101st Congress, the geographic distribution of the Enterprisers differed from the total party distribution (the geographic distribution of each faction does not shift much between congresses). Enterpriser Republicans were rare from Maine through Virginia. They were dominant in the Pacific states, and strong in the South and the Plains/Rocky Mountain region.

The timing of this faction's emergence and its geographical distribution highlight the connection of this faction to prominent issues in the Reagan-Bush era. Pacific lawmakers were drawn to Enterpriser-like behavior through Reagan the Californian. In addition, the Enterpriser dominance in the Plains/Rockies and the Pacific highlights the faction's mixture of strong economic conservatism combined with some measure of libertarian thinking that government ought to stay out of personal morality. This geographical mix reinforces the impression that this faction favors a consistent "limited government" ideology for domestic issues. In the 104th Congress, several members of the GOP leadership and other prominent Republicans are Enterprisers. Speaker Newt Gingrich is an Enterpriser. The Georgian, who began his House career in 1979, has been the impetus behind the House GOP tactical and policy agenda that eventually brought Republicans majority status. Tactically, he led the charge to advance House GOP interests through the media, through candidate recruitment and support, and through grassroots organizations such as GOPAC, shunning traditional legislative work to gain personal and party influence in the House. Another Enterpriser is House Majority Leader Dick Armey of Texas who, only ten years after winning his House seat, was unanimously named by his colleagues in late 1994 as Majority Leader. Armey's rise differed from Gingrich, although both pursued confrontational politics hostile to the leadership of both parties. While Gingrich's confrontation focused on the media, the broad framework of policy, and congressional ethics, Armey focused on policy, especially in economics. He turned a last-minute January 1991 appointment as ranking House Republican on the Joint Economic Committee (offered as a consolation prize by Republican Leader Bob Michel for not being named ranking Republican on the House Budget Committee) into the central congressional platform for pro-growth economics. His success in defending growth-oriented economic policy and spreading its arguments to House Republicans and congressional candidates pushed him quickly up the formal leadership ladder.

A closer examination of the intellectual influences of Gingrich and Armey help to illustrate the similarities and differences in the Enterpriser faction. Gingrich is the futurist and global strategist, holding together an eclectic set of intellectual ideas gleaned from his training in history and his interest in science fiction. Gingrich earned a Ph.D. in history from Tulane University, and taught for a few years at Georgia State College before launching an early political career. From his formal educational background he sees himself as something of an expert in military history and strategy, and inevitably views most of his political battles and challenges with a mind to historical parallels. And at least since his early years in the House, he has been fascinated with the scientific and technological possibilities of the future and the impact of these changes on the government, the economy, and private life. As such, especially in the last few years he has sought out friendships with futurists Alvin and Heidi Toffler and management gurus Edward Deming and Peter Drucker.

The combination of old values and new technology creates a unique "futuristic conservatism" that embraces technological change simultaneously with old-fashioned American moral, familial, and entrepreneurial sentiments. This eclectic mix is then surrounded by almost unbridled optimism about the American future. The result is a highly energetic vision of a futuristic America with a far smaller central government but a far more pleasing and satisfying life for its citizens.

Fellow Enterpriser Armey is as optimistic about America's future as Gingrich is, but for vastly different reasons. If Gingrich is the futuristic conservative appealing to high-tech aficionados, Armey is the classical libertarian conservative who finds a warm place in the heart of the working man. While Gingrich trusts what he sees in the future, Armey trusts what he has learned about the past. Armey also has a PhD; his is in economics from the University of Oklahoma. He taught his specialty in a series of self-described "bush-league" colleges, mostly in Texas. In the late 1970s and early 1980s at North Texas State (now the University of North Texas) Armey became quite a popular local speaker on economic issues, espousing the libertarian views of his hero Milton Friedman. Since coming to the House in 1985, Armey has developed and maintained the rather remarkable simultaneous reputations of intellectual, loner, and effective legislator. His best-known legislative effort was to push through Congress a defense base-closing bill to shield the necessary military downsizing from congressional politicking and log-rolling. He is a firm believer that less government is better, trusting far more in "the goodness of the American people than the guile of the American government." This learned libertarian optimism in the creative individual is tempered a bit by an experienced social policy conservatism that relies on "the influence of family, the weight of tradition, and above all religious conviction" to form the virtuous lives under which a more limited government is feasible.[2]

Armey's combination of intellectual libertarianism with practical, almost folksy, social conservatism is far more representative of Enterpriser thinking than is Gingrich's futurism. Armey's views are a better base upon which to reach out to other factions such as Moralists and more passive conservatives, but less useful in creating the dynamic party realignment that Enterprisers seek. As a complementary vision, Gingrich's views appeal to more moderate factions in the House, and potentially to a wider public seeking solutions for a new and more complicated post-industrial era. The intellectualism and optimism of Gingrich and Armey, although stemming from different sources, are common to them and to the entire Enterpriser faction. Intellectualism has respectability in the Washington policy environment; optimism surrounding individualistic American values helps to justify shrinking government power in the face of growing complexity of contemporary events.

Other Enterprisers in the 104th Congress include GOP Policy Committee Chairman Christopher Cox of California; Rules Committee member David Dreier of California, who played a leadership role in congressional reorganization; and Bill McCollum of Florida, who was a leader on congressional term limits. Several Enterprisers served during the Reagan-Bush era, but were no longer members when the party became the majority. Jack Kemp of New York left the House in 1988 in a failed presidential bid; Dick Cheney of Wyoming left in 1989 to become secretary of defense; Trent Lott won a Senate seat in 1988 and became Senate Republican Whip in the 104th Congress; and Mickey Edwards, who chaired the House Research and Policy Committees, lost his seat in a primary because of the House banking scandal.

The data for this study shed further light on Enterprisers. Table 4.4 shows that Enterprisers are consistently conservative voters. Although they are not quite the most conservative faction overall, they are among the most conservative tenth of all representatives on all *NJ* votes, and they are the most conservative faction on *NJ* economic votes.

The purpose of table 4.4, the voting profile table, is to compare the texture of a faction's voting record with the texture of other factions and of all House Republicans. The objective is to identify differences in issue emphasis that are obscured if only one or a few voting measures are used. High *NJ* economic and foreign policy scores and high National Taxpayers Union scores suggest that Enterprisers are extremely conservative on these issues, which President Reagan emphasized and which again became prominent in the 104th Congress as Republicans took charge. In addition, although Enterprisers are conservative on social policy, that conservatism appears less extreme than in the other two issue areas.

A unidimensional scale might place Enterprisers to the right of the House Republican mainstream. The more detailed analysis here, however, indicates that their conservatism is distinct and somewhat at variance with a New Right/religious right agenda. Enterpriser intellectual and policy arguments originate with neoconservatives, free-market economists, and their associated think tanks in Washington, D.C. Current Enterpriser leaders are favorites with many of these think tanks. Armey is closely associated with the neoconservative Heritage Foundation, and the more libertarian Cato Institute and Citizens for a Sound Economy. He formally supports many of their efforts, and in recent years has hired key staff persons from each organization. Gingrich also works closely with these groups, although he tends to set up new organizations, such as the Progress and Freedom Foundation, to work more directly on issues of his immediate concern.

Also collected for this study are the typical committee assignments for members of each faction, as table 4.5 illustrates. While the differences here between the GOP mean and the Enterprisers are modest, these differences do not contradict the general impression of Enterprisers as more interested than the average Republican House member in policy matters, and less interested in constituency concerns.

Additional information collected for this study focuses on the activity levels. Specifically, the study collects data on party committee memberships, legislative activity as measured by bills sponsored and cosponsored, and a national activity score that is a combination of policy-oriented memberships in standing committees, party committees, and caucuses. These scores provide further evidence of the Enterpriser interest in national policy issues. First, the typical Enterpriser belongs to more than three party committees (these include the Policy Committee, Research Committee, Campaign Committee, and various Leader or Research Committee task forces). The typical Enterpriser is slightly more active on legislation than the typical GOP member, and far more active on the combined national score, which takes into account all types of committee and caucus memberships.

The final table on each faction, table 4.7, is based on caucus membership data. It examines the specific caucus memberships of each Republican member, and groups those memberships into the three categories of intraparty caucuses, nationally oriented caucuses, and locally oriented caucuses. These data serve to reinforce the tendency of Enterprisers to be active in national policy. The typical Enterpriser is a member of 2.0 national caucuses, while the GOP average is around 1.5. In addition, Enterprisers have fewer local caucus membership than the typical House GOP member (these scores range from just over 1.0 to just under 2.0). At the same time, total Enterpriser caucus membership is above the mean, and higher than all other factions except the Moderates and Patricians. Enterprisers have about the same proportion of intraparty caucuses memberships as the entire party.

In sum, the picture of Enterprisers the data presents includes several broad lines. First, many of the faction's scores are close to the House GOP mean, suggesting that Enterprisers would not stand out as a faction under a cursory review of House Republicans. Second, in most policy areas, the voting record of Enterprisers lies on the conservative side of a conservative party, but not quite at the extreme.

Activity measures, which are attempts to measure attitudes toward traditional norms and issues, more clearly identify Enterprisers. One expects Enterprisers to be less supportive of traditional norms, and more interested in sweeping reforms and partisan political activity. Under Democratic rule, many Enterprisers introduced comprehensive legislative packages that were at once sweeping and impractical under the prevailing congressional regime. Enterprisers rose quickly to prominence in the middle and later Reagan years, as national prosperity seemed to confirm the wisdom of Reagan economic policy.

Their style of legislative activity indicates that Enterprisers do not distrust congressional lawmaking *per se*, so much as they disliked its course during Democratic rule. As their support for Gingrich as Whip indicated, when in the minority Enterprisers were likely to support a stronger and more partisan House GOP. In addition, Enterprisers were more likely to believe that an identifiable domestic agenda was important to their own and to the party's congressional electoral success. In many ways, the 1994 election results indicate that the Enterprisers' beliefs, adopted by the House leadership for that campaign, were the key to GOP House majority status.

Moralists

Moralists are the second conservative policy-oriented faction. As the name implies, they are identified by conservatism on social issue voting, and generally back the agenda of social conservatives. Election-year gains as shown in table 4.2 suggest that Moralists grew in the early 1980s, benefitting from both the 1982 and 1984 elections. In addition, the 1994 elections may have brought in another large influx of Moralists, as many in the freshman GOP class had much in common with the Moralist profile, especially their geographic origins and professional backgrounds outside of public service.

The Moralists are now the largest policy-oriented faction, and usually compose about 20 percent of the conference. Table 4.3 portrays the regional dispersion of the faction. Moralists are rare in New England and the Mid-Atlantic states and prominent in the South and the Pacific. Moralists are more dominant than Enterprisers in the

South and less dominant in the Pacific states. The two most represented Moralist states are Texas and California. In addition, some Moralists are from the Border states, with cultures similar to that of Deep South states. The geographical dispersion of Moralists suggests that the faction tilts toward southern and western Republicanism and the social conservatism of those regions.

Several prominent House Republicans are or were consistent members of the Moralist faction. House leaders in the 104th Congress identified as Moralists include GOP Whip Tom DeLay of Texas and Conference Chair John Boehner of Ohio. Other reasonably well-known Moralists in the 104th Congress include Phil Crane of Illinois; Robert Dornan of California known for his rhetorical flourishes on several conservative social issues; Dan Burton of Indiana; and Randall "Duke" Cunningham of California, who was very active in opposing attempts by the Clinton administration to end the prohibition of open homosexuals serving in the military. Other Moralists who left the House before the 104th Congress include John Ashbrook of Ohio, a strongly conservative activist; Mark Siljander of Michigan who was very active in the pro-life movement but lost his seat after associating his 1986 primary opponent with "the forces of Satan"; and Bill Dannemeyer of California, who lost his 1992 attempt to move to the U.S. Senate.

Table 4.4 illustrates the issue-voting profile of the policy factions in the 101st Congress. On nearly all measures the Moralist faction scored as the most conservative GOP group. Their *NJ* mean score of 7.42 is the most conservative by far. The Moralist social and foreign policy scores are also the most conservative. But their economic policy scores are not as conservative as Enterprisers. Moralists have slightly lower *NJ* economic scores, a far smaller fiscal conservatism ratio that is at the GOP mean, and NTU scores only slightly more conservative than Enterprisers (and Stalwarts). These scores may indicate that socially conservative Moralists are not necessarily the most fiscally conservative voters, perhaps because social conservatism is distributed all along the income scale. Some Moralists represent economically strained areas that depend upon specific federal projects or major federal welfare programs. These Moralists would support these programs, or at least oppose the most ambitious plans to cut them, while still voting solidly for a conservative social agenda. Moralists who have this characteristic include Jim Bunning of Kentucky and Tom Bliley of Virginia. A social conservative from a lower-middle-class district may have somewhat more liberal views about the proper role of government in domestic economic matters. In general, however, Moralist conservatism extends to all areas.

A unidimensional scale would identify Moralists as "hard-core" conservatives. The several measures used here add helpful nuances. Moralists are especially conservative on social and foreign issues, but their slightly more liberal economic score may indicate a touch of populism and adjustment to intermittent harsh economic times in their districts.

Committee membership data from table 4.5 show sharp contrasts between the Moralist and Enterpriser factions. First, few Moralists serve on influence committees; the 0.18 score is as low as any faction. Second, their placement on constituency committees is far higher than any other faction, likely a reflection of their more junior status (in most Congresses they are the most junior group of members) as constituency committees tend to be the largest, least requested committees whose many open slots are left for junior members. Finally, their policy committee memberships are also the lowest of any policy faction, and lower than all other factions except the Placeholders. The committee profile can also be explained by the discomfort the Old Guard leadership experienced with the Moralist issue agenda. The Old Guard was certainly socially conservative, but few were willing to make social issues the centerpiece of House Republican policy, especially in a Democratic House where there would be no hope of success.

The activity-level data from table 4.6 also indicate that Moralists have a different style from the Enterprisers, even though their voting patterns are similar. The average Moralist is only on 1.35 party committees, the fewest of all but one other faction (Placeholders), and their national activity score of 3.64 is far lower than the party mean of 5.23 and lower than all but the same faction. This data indicate that Moralists are less interested than Enterprisers in building a broad majority-party coalition focused on national issues.

The final data, from table 4.7, portray caucus memberships. Here again Moralists are fairly inactive, except on local caucuses. They belong to about half as many national caucuses as Enterprisers, about the same number of intraparty groups, and slightly more local caucuses than Enterprisers and the GOP mean.

The Moralists' voting conservatism and behavioral inaction lead to one of two conclusions. On the one hand, Moralists may have very little interest in the traditional ways of doing business, especially within the post-reform Democratic House. On the other hand, the low influence committee score may indicate that Moralists offended older established leadership Republicans, who during most of the post-reform era played the decisive role in naming members to influence committees.

The picture of Moralists in this analysis has several details. First, Moralists are the most conservative faction, especially on domestic social issues and on defense matters. In these key areas, the Moralist position in the Reagan-Bush period defined the right-wing position on issues within the House Republican conference. In economic policy, they betray some populist leanings.

Activity measures for Moralists are low. A plausible explanation for this activity pattern is that Moralists are interested in only the set of issues that defines the extreme foreign and social policy right, and that in the Reagan-Bush era they looked to Republican presidents for positional and voting cues on these issues.

Moralists were probably content with the ideological direction of the national GOP in the early and mid-1980s, and saw little need to distinguish themselves from President Reagan. As a consequence, most Moralists were not active in the traditional legislative or policy-making process dominated by Democrats and more moderate GOP factions. This passivity is especially apparent for Moralists from the South and West, who seemed to ride comfortably the coattails of the Reagan agenda. In fact, the distinction between the passivity of these Moralists, from the far greater activity of northern and eastern Moralists, suggests a division within the faction on the basis of geography. Most Sunbelt Moralists do not appear to be closely tied to national social movement groups. Rather, they reflect a regional cultural conservatism that became more prominent during the 1980s. Some Sunbelt Moralists have political biographies similar to Stalwarts, who are more supportive of institutions and norms. Eight of the eleven Moralist votes for Madigan in the 1989 Whip race were cast by Californians or southerners, with Moralist Tom DeLay of Texas working hard for Madigan in that race. Gingrich received almost twice as many Moralist votes as Madigan, but the winner received only eight faction votes from California and the South. In contrast, Gingrich won twelve faction votes from the Plains/Rockies, Midwest, and Mid-Atlantic, compared with one for Madigan.

Moralists outside the South and West frequently associate with groups tied to issues of anticommunism or domestic social problems. Mark Siljander, for example, earned a narrow plurality in a crowded 1981 primary special election, and won subsequent primaries in 1982 and 1984.[3] During his tenure in Congress, Siljander launched a series of initiatives on moral issues, including a drive to proclaim 1982 as the "Year of the Unborn Child." Siljander claimed to be the most outspoken member of Congress on abortion, homosexuality, and, in his words, "general moral-type issues." His behavior was only the most prominent of that of a dozen or so Snowbelt Moralists. Phil Crane, an older Moralist from Illinois, is closely tied to traditional conservative groups such as the American Conservative Union, of which he served as chair for many years.

The influence of the Moralist faction on Republican politics in the Reagan-Bush era was smaller than their numerical strength in the House GOP conference indicates. Few Moralists with moral constituencies, mostly the Snowbelt Moralists, sustained public support. Many who emphasized this narrow base lost either to other Republicans or to Democrats, or narrowly maintained their seats. Siljander, Dan Crane of Illinois, Donald "Buz" Lukens of Ohio, and others ran into trouble with the high standards of behavior that their Moralist issue stands implied. A second reason why Moralists had little influence is their focus on personal behavior over legislative accomplishment. For example, in the 101st Congress, Jim Inhofe of Oklahoma and Chuck Douglas of New Hampshire criticized the homosexuality of Massachusetts representative Barney Frank as relevant to his fitness for office.[4] Such attacks violated a congressional norm shared even by many very conservative Republicans. It also invited their opponents to hold them to a far higher level of individual scrutiny. In addition, this interest in the personal behavior of other members, and the centrality of that focus to their view of the job of representation led to relative inactivity. Such motivations offer no impetus for Moralists to advance legislative agendas or pursue leadership in the House, or for the GOP leadership to advance Moralist careers.

Moralists are now part of the House GOP leadership for the first time, mostly because of their growing numbers in the Conference. Before the 1994 elections, Bill Dannemeyer was the only Moralist who had ever seriously run for a House leadership position. His try was an embarrassing failure, as he received seven votes in a 1988 bid to become chairman of the House Republican Conference.[5]

Moralists had little success in pushing the small subset of directly religious issues, such as prayer in public schools, abortion, and homosexuality, which are their characteristic concerns. While a majority of Republicans may agree with those positions, few put them at the top of a national policy agenda. The September 1994 House GOP "Contract With America" carefully avoided Moralist issues in order to appeal to the greatest number of voters. The GOP contract was compiled by House Republican leaders and pushed through the House in fewer than the 100 days promised. But the May 1995 Christian Coalition "Contract with the American Family" gained a politely positive response from most House GOP leaders, but no pledges of floor consideration by a certain date.

Traditionally there is broader support in the conference for conservative cultural issues such as attacking affirmative action, getting tough on crime and drugs, lowering taxes, reducing spending, and loosening government regulations. Many Moralists focus on these issues, and these issues provide opportunities for Moralists to join with other House Republican factions, especially Enterprisers, to bring them to the attention of the public and place them high on the congressional agenda. All these broader issues except affirmative action were addressed in the 1994 Contract With America, and in the early 104th Congress the latter was being primed as a major party issue for the 1996 contest.

This cooperation between Moralists and Enterprisers was a central element to the Contract With America. Moralist hostility to dominant cultural values and Enterpriser hostility to dominant policy alternatives were central motivations of the legislative proposals of the Contract With America.

Also important to the contract was congressional reform, which tapped into the hostility of the House GOP to the perceived procedural unfairness of the House Democratic majority. These procedural issues were somewhat important to policy-oriented conservatives, but they were critical to the policy-oriented House GOP factions to be considered next—the Moderates and Patricians.

Moderate Policy-Oriented Factions: Moderates and Patricians

Moderates are far less ideological or comprehensive than either conservative faction in attacking contemporary culture or policy. And Patricians are far removed from their fellow party members on policy issues and partisan feeling. But as Democratic partisanship created a hostile House climate by the mid-1980s, these GOP factions began to find more in common with their very conservative party colleagues.

The growth of frustration, which helped to overcome the ideological doubts about Gingrich, is reflected in the vote totals of these moderate policy-oriented factions for Gingrich in the 1989 Whip race. The Moderate faction, close to Madigan in voting style but more frustrated than he by the partisanship of the House, actually gave Gingrich twelve out of its twenty votes. Patricians gave him four out of its eleven votes. Of these two factions' combined thirty-one votes, Gingrich obtained a majority of one—a reasonable share based upon this analysis but one few would expect based upon a mere comparison of unidimensional voting scores.

The labels for these factions are chosen, like the Enterpriser and Moralist labels, to imply several characteristics. "Moderate," of course, first implies placement in the middle of voting scales. The typical Moderate GOP member is slightly more liberal than the average House Republican and slightly more conservative than the average House member. In this study, the *NJ* mean score of Moderates is 38 (in the 101st Congress), compared with 21.3 for the House GOP and 50 for the entire House. The second implication of the term is its nonideological content. House Moderates prefer incremental modifications to current courses. These are perfect predispositions to work in a Congress controlled by either party—as long as the controlling party is not too partisan or ideological. While they are activists, Moderates like to pursue policy goals over partisan objectives and are more active in legislative and national policy caucuses, especially those that pursue active policy agendas.

The term "Patrician" has social and economic implications. First, it suggests a sense of *noblesse oblige* that may border on paternalism, and it also implies a sense of economic generosity. In addition, the term suggests a person with manners and respect for tradition. In politics, a Patrician can be expected to be generous with federal programs and dollars, and to respect institutions and norms, especially norms of civilized conduct and bipartisan comity. Patricians may feel disdain for partisanship. In the post-reform House, they would avoid a hostile attitude toward Democratic partisanship as long as possible, even though they may agree with most of the conservative activist critique of the institution.

Moderates

Moderates have longer tenure in the House GOP than Enterprisers or Moralists, and are more geographically concentrated. Under the methodology of this analysis, their numbers have also increased rather than decreased during the Reagan-Bush era. But because of the sharp decline among Patricians, House GOP policy in the Reagan-Bush era has become dominated by conservatives.

Table 4.2 illustrates the relative size of each faction in the 1980s and beyond. In that table, Moderates fare quite well, growing from 5.7 percent of the party in the 97th Congress of 1981–82, to 10.8 percent of the House GOP by the 103rd Congress. The biggest change in their relative numbers was early in the period, as in the 98th Congress of 1983–84 Moderate numbers had already grown to nearly 10 percent of the conference.

Moderates are concentrated by region, as table 4.3 illustrates. In the model 101st Congress, 40 percent (twelve of twenty) of Moderates were from the Mid-Atlantic states and 25 percent were from the Midwest. This geographic concentration suggests, however, several reasons for the moderate voting record of this group. First is the relative longevity of the GOP in these regions. As Howard Reiter hypothesized, moderate to liberal "Misfit" members of the GOP may be centered in older areas of party dominance since they would find few reasons to become recent converts to the GOP.

The roster of Moderates in the 104th Congress includes many "pragmatic" or "thoughtful" Republicans traditionally applauded in standard Washington, D.C., media and punditry circles. Moderates include Nancy Johnson of Connecticut, who has become active in health care reform; Jim Leach of Iowa, who has worked on campaign reform; John Porter of Illinois, who spent the early part of the 104th Congress protecting public broadcasting and family planning services; Christopher Shays of Connecticut, who has been active in urban policy; and Steve Gunderson of Wisconsin, who has been active in agricultural policy and increasingly outspoken in urging GOP tolerance of homosexuals.

The roster of Moderates no longer serving by 1995 reads like a list of recent GOP statewide candidates. Gubernatorial aspirants include Fred Grandy of Iowa, Tom Ridge of Pennsylvania, Ron Machtley of Rhode Island, and John McKernan of Maine. Successful or at least aspiring senators include Olympia Snowe of Maine, Lynn Martin of Illinois, Tom Tauke of Iowa, Rod Chandler of Washington, and Tom Campbell of California.

The biographies of several current and former Moderates suggest that most of the faction is interested in constructive policy alternatives. Tauke, Porter, Martin, and Bill Frenzel of Minnesota are called thoughtful, independent, and accomplished in a popular almanac of

U.S. representatives.[6] Biographies in such almanacs tend to reward conventional views. The favorable comments about Moderates indicate that the group includes many "responsible" positional conservatives, preferred by supporters of the institutional status quo and Washington purveyors of conventional wisdom.

Table 4.4 shows the voting pattern of each faction, and this information for the Moderates suggests that the faction contains elements of "Main Street" sentiments and, perhaps, a strain of libertarianism on domestic issues. The faction's *NJ* mean score is 38, above the House GOP mean and more moderate than the Enterpriser/Moralist range. At the same time, that score is far more conservative than the Patrician average of 57.5. Policy scores suggest greater Moderate conservatism on economic issues. First, the Moderate *NJ* economic score is 31.25, above the GOP mean of 20.3 but far closer to it than to the overall average. In addition, this faction's NTU score is 69.3, near the GOP mean of 73.6. At the same time, Moderate scores on foreign policy and social policy are far higher at 38.35 and 44.5, respectively.

These data point to a libertarian-like resistance on the part of Moderates to social conservatives on issues such as school prayer, abortion, and homosexual rights. Not every Moderate, of course, is a libertarian. Representative Tom Tauke of Iowa, for example, was strongly pro-life. Other Moderates have fairly conservative *NJ* foreign policy scores. However, the general view of limited government in these areas is reflected in the Moderate pattern of *NJ* social, foreign, and economic policy scores.

Moderates have a unique pattern of committee membership. No other policy faction is more active on policy or influence committees, or less active on constituency committees. The pattern reflects both Moderate interest in the policy environment and their relatively long tenure. At 0.75, the number of policy committees per typical Moderate is far higher than any other faction. The number of influence committee memberships per Moderate is also the highest for any policy group. The number of constituency committees, however, is far below any other faction. These figures indicate that Moderates are interested in policy and were, at least during the Reagan-Bush era, trusted by fellow insiders in the old House GOP leadership.

Moderates are slightly more active than the typical Republican on party committees and in general legislative activity. In addition, their total national activity score is far above the GOP mean and twice that of the Moralists. Throughout the era, many Moderates displayed these legislative interests. Nancy Johnson of Connecticut has been very active in many areas of legislation, but specifically in health care and urban problems. William Goodling of Pennsylvania, as ranking member on the Education and Labor Committee and now chairman of the renamed "Opportunities" Committee, focused most of his efforts on secondary education policy. John Porter of Illinois actively promotes public broadcasting, abortion rights, and private voluntary organizations. Steve Gunderson of Wisconsin devotes a great deal of energy to agricultural policy, especially the dairy interests of his district, and educational policy.

The aggregate picture allows us to draw several conclusions about the Moderate faction. First, although unidimensional measures of voting would put Moderates slightly left of the average House GOP member, a closer analysis indicates that the faction is more complex. The distinguishing voting pattern is permissiveness on social and foreign policy issues but restraint on the size of government.

Activity measures reveal several special distinctions between Moderates and Enterprisers. First, while Enterprisers are policy oriented, Moderates have more memberships on the key policy and influence committees and indicate even greater interest in policy. Moderate legislative and national activity levels and total caucus membership levels are far higher than those of the more conservative policy groups. All this evidence suggests that during the Reagan-Bush era Moderates were reasonably comfortable in the congressional policymaking environment, at least until late in the period when House Democrats began regularly and completely to shut faction members out of the policymaking process. Based on their interests, Moderates were likely the faction most offended and discouraged by the growing partisanship of the late post-reform House.

Patricians

Patricians are the most liberal of the House GOP policy-oriented factions, and the one that experienced the greatest numerical decline in the Reagan-Bush era. As table 4.2 shows, Patricians composed 14.1 percent of the House GOP Conference in the 97th Congress of 1981–82, but only 1.1 percent of the party's House members in the 103rd Congress of 1993–94. Losses were in two big steps—after the 1982 elections when Patricians numbers fell to 6 percent and after the 1990 elections when they fell to 3 percent.

As will be shown later, this decline occurred for two reasons. First, many Patricians left the House in the Reagan-Bush era and were replaced either by Republicans of differing views or by Democrats. Second, Patrician members of earlier congresses migrated to either the Moderate or Placeholder groups, voting more conservatively and falling below the 50 percent *NJ* mean cut-off.

The geographic distribution in table 4.3 indicates the Patricians, like Moderates, are centered in a few geographic areas. For the 101st Congress, about 46 percent of Patricians came from the Mid-Atlantic, and an almost equal percentage from New England. No Patrician was from the South, Pacific, or Plains/Rocky states. If there is a geographically isolated House GOP faction in the current era, it is the Patrician.

Patrician numbers have dwindled so severely since 1980 that it seems almost futile to list the most prominent members of the group. Only Connie Morella of Maryland was clearly in the Patrician group in the 103rd Congress, although many other members of that Congress were labeled as Patricians in earlier Congresses. Included among that group are latter-day Moderates Jim Leach of Iowa, Christopher Shays and Nancy Johnson of Connecticut, Olympia Snowe of Maine, and Hamilton Fish of New York. In addition, a few former Patricians later came to be classified as constituency-oriented Placeholders, including Marge Roukema of New Jersey, and Ben Gilman and Sherwood Boehlert of New York. Former members of the Patrician faction who left Congress before 1994 include Bill Green and Frank Horton of New York; Silvio Conte of Massachusetts; Claudine Schneider of Rhode Island; Jim Jeffords of Vermont; Stewart McKinney and Larry DeNardis of Connecticut; and a host of New Jersey representatives including Harold Hollenbeck, Millicent Fenwick, and Matthew Rinaldo. Very early in the Reagan-Bush era a few Patricians popped up in other areas, including Arlen Erdahl in Minnesota and Pete McCloskey in California.

This list of Patricians provides several items of interest. First is the unusual migration by members out of this faction. This phenomenon can be expected upon observing that the *NJ* mean score for House Republicans fell from about twenty-nine in the 97th Congress to about twenty-two in the 98th Congress and down to about nineteen in 1994. This fall in the average GOP score would almost require fewer Patricians. What is surprising is the precipitous fall marked by 1982. That year nine Patricians left the House, and fully one-third of 1981–82 Patricians moved into the more conservative Moderate or Placeholder factions. None moved the other way, to a more liberal voting record.

The voting pattern of Patricians also highlights their distinctiveness.

In the 101st Congress, Patricians were the least conservative group in all three *National Journal* issue areas, and were especially liberal in social and foreign policy—their respective scores of 67.9 and 58.7 are more than twenty points more liberal than the closest group, the Moderates.

The Patrician economic dimension score of 44.8 is by a good margin still in the conservative half of the total House. In addition, the Patrician NTU spending score is also 53.2, slightly more positive than negative in the view of that interest group. Although they are permissive on social issues and cautious in foreign affairs, Patricians are still relatively tight-fisted. Where Patricians clearly deviate from Republican orthodoxy is in social and foreign policy. Their extremely low scores underline the growing separation of Patricians from the mainstream of Republicans increasingly influenced by Moralists and Enterprisers.

A unidimensional voting scale distinguishes Patricians from other House Republicans. Such a scale, however, misses nuances such as the group's relative economic conservatism and its direct conflict with Republican orthodoxy on domestic social and foreign policy issues. The more complex analysis used here clarifies the distinctive Patrician liberalism. This point of view can be characterized as broadly consonant with libertarian ideas of social liberalism, foreign policy noninterventionism, and relatively tight-fisted economics.

The fiscal conservatism ratio, heretofore not particularly useful in explaining House GOP factionalism, also reveals a plausible reason that Patricians remain Republicans and do not become Democrats. *National Journal* scores are relative to all members of Congress, and House Republicans as a conference are relatively more conservative on economic issues. Consequently, House Democrats as a caucus must be more liberal on economic policy than foreign or social policy, and have an average fiscal conservative ratio below 1.0. Therefore, although Patricians might on a unidimensional scale look like moderately conservative Democrats, the Patrician Republican pattern of voting across the three areas is the inverse of conservative Democrats, who would vote relatively conservatively on defense and social policy and relatively liberally on taxing and spending issues. This different texture of voting does much to explain why it is difficult for moderate Republicans to join with conservative Democrats in a lasting and effective middle-of-the-road congressional coalition, even though there have been several attempts over the years and new attempts in the 104th Republican Congress.

The committee data illustrated in table 4.5 do not really distinguish the Patrician faction from the GOP. Patricians have a slightly higher tendency than the average House Republican to be on a policy committee, but they are far behind the Moderates on this score. In addition, Patrician representation on constituency committees is slightly above the GOP mean, but the faction's representation on influence committees is far lower than the mean—in fact exactly equal to the Moralists' 0.18 per member. The Patrician level on these committees is about half that of Moderates, and about two-thirds that of the conference as a whole.

Patricians are the most active House Republican faction, however. Their legislative activity ratio is 1.38, the highest of any faction. In addition, their national activity score is 7.55, high above the GOP mean and higher than any other faction. Twice as often as the average House Republican, and far more than any other group, Patricians join in national caucuses. In addition, Patricians are far more likely to be members of intraparty groups (the Wednesday Group and the '92 Group in this case) and even slightly more likely to be part of local-oriented caucuses. Clearly, the Patrician faction is an activist, policy-oriented group.

The Patrician interest in issues could explain their high legislative activity, and the score probably indicates support for the traditional legislative norms of the House. In addition, because the Patricians' issue agenda and their positions on these issues differ from that of most other Republicans, faction members are those expected to be most willing to work with Democrats and with each other on policy initiatives, and less frequently with other Republicans.

Findings from the measures used in this analysis imply several things. First, nearly every measure shows the Patricians' unique position. This group is the most liberal, the most active, the most bipartisan, and the most geographically distinct faction. They may also be the most threatened by extinction. Most Patricians come from areas in which the GOP has done poorly in recent elections. Extinction, however, is unlikely given that several former Patricians remain in the House as Moderates and Placeholders, probably voting more conservatively in the latter years of the extremely partisan Democratic House and, at least so far, in the early stages of Republican control.

Because of their predisposition to bipartisanship, Patricians may have had the largest and most negative reaction to the takeover of hostility in the House. Even more used to bipartisanship and participation than the Moderates, Patricians may have been expected to react even more strongly against the growing exclusivity and partisanship of House Democratic leaders in the 1980s and early 1990s. While in earlier years Patricians adapted to the congressional environment in ways distinct from other House Republicans, most prominently by continued cooperation with Democrats at the risk of alienating GOP leaders, that option became increasingly closed off as the Reagan-Bush era continued.

Patrician cooperation with Democrats gave some issues a misleading aura of bipartisanship, one that may have been resented by other Republicans, especially the conservative and partisan Enterprisers and Moralists. Patrician-led opposition to many Reagan positions created the impression of Republican disunity, which harms minority parties in legislatures more than majority parties. Patrician opposition was not uncommon, even on the most crucial elements of Republican policy, during the early 1980s.

Patrician cooperation with Democrats may have been the consequence of individual decisions that such a strategy was the best way to bring home local projects. Patrician bipartisan cooperation may also reflect a belief that "good policy makes good politics." This latter attitude appears to have been widespread among Patricians. For example, Hamilton Fish made major contributions to fair housing and immigration reform legislation in his service on the Judiciary Committee.[7] Ben Gilman, Frank Horton, and Jim Leach were also well-known and frequently applauded for their bipartisan approach to legislating, with Gilman and Leach both very active in foreign affairs, and the latter strongly supportive of campaign reform legislation usually promoted by Democrats.[8]

Whatever the motivation, Patrician bipartisan cooperation has its negative side: alienation from the spreading Republican conservative activism of the 1980s. Indeed, the development of the Ripon Society in the 1970s, the "gypsy moths" in 1981 to resist the Reagan budget cuts, and the '92 Group in 1985 can all be seen as attempts to resist a growing conservative force in the party.

This overwhelming Patrician tendency toward bipartisan cooperation slowly was overcome in the later years of the post-reform era. The growing excesses in closed and complex rules and the rough treatment by House Democrats of a more Patrician-like President Bush evidently pushed even some Patricians into a more confrontational opposition stance. While more hesitant than Moderates to give up on bipartisan cooperation, Patricians came to see the merits of joining with other Republicans in strongly supporting the 1994 Contract With

America strategy. Some Patricians or former Patricians, most notably Shays of Connecticut, campaigned aggressively for the contract despite its strong economic conservatism.

Summary

The issues emphasized in the 1980s affected moderate policy-oriented groups in several ways. On the one hand, renewed GOP interest in substantive issues, measured by a general rise in policy-oriented members, encouraged Moderates and Patricians who have long sought to play constructive roles in the legislative process. Most Moderates and even some Patricians could join in constructive legislative projects with less doctrinaire Enterprisers.

Specifically, there are two common interests shared by all policy-oriented House Republican factions. First, all four seek an effective legislative body that passes coherent initiatives. Toward that end, all policy-oriented Republican groups could criticize the alleged partisanship of the Democratic majority, the incrementalism of most legislation, and the inefficiency of government that became more of a public issue in the early 1990s. Differences about policy agendas mask the second common interest among these four factions, which is a more "responsible" Republican party, as defined in the academic literature, united against Democratic partisanship in support of a Republican House.

The new House Republican leaders of the mid-1990s managed to hold together this "hostile coalition" dedicated to confronting Democratic rule. To the cultural hostility of Moralists and the policy hostility of Enterprisers was added the procedural hostility of many Moderates and even some Patricians. This coalition was deftly managed by Gingrich and Armey in compiling the Contract With America for the 1994 congressional campaign, putting procedural issues at the front of the contract as "first-day" reforms necessary to clean up the institution before policy change was tackled.

Notes

1. Steven S. Smith and Christopher J. Deering, *Committees in Congress*, 2nd ed. (Washington, D.C.: Congressional Quarterly Press, 1990), 87.

2. Paul Starobin, "True Believer," *National Journal* 27 (7 January 1995): 8–13.

3. Michael Barone and Grant Ujifusa, *Almanac of American Politics 1986* (Washington, D.C.: National Journal, 1985), 668.

4. Phil Duncan, ed., *Congressional Quarterly's Politics in America 1990: the 101st Congress* (Washington, D.C.: Congressional Quarterly, 1989), 1217 and 923.

5. Michael Barone and Grant Ujifusa, *Almanac of American Politics 1990* (Washington, D.C.: National Journal, 1989), 212.

6. See in Duncan, *Politics 1990*, the biographies of Tauke, 534–36; Porter, 446–48; Martin, 463–65; and Frenzel, 795–97.

7. Barone, *Almanac 1990*, 856.

8. See in Duncan, *Politics 1990*, biographies of Gilman, 1057; and Horton, 1076.

Chapter 5

Constituency-Oriented House Republican Factions

Constituency-oriented representatives account for approximately half the House Republicans. This chapter identifies and analyzes the three constituency-oriented factions in the party—Stalwarts, Provincials, and Placeholders—in the same manner as the policy-oriented factions were examined in the previous chapter.

As noted previously, the distinction between a representative's interest in policy issues or constituency matters is common in congressional research. The dividing line in this analysis is legislative activity, placing those members with above-average legislative activity into policy-oriented groups, and those with below-average legislative activity into constituency-oriented groups. This is, of course, an imperfect division. Policy activists might not be active legislatively, especially if these activists viewed the legislative process in a Democratic House as essentially illegitimate. Conversely, constituency-oriented members may be active in seeking particularistic benefits for local constituents. As such, the labels do not capture all the nuances of the basic division. Alternatively, policy activists could easily be categorized as national-issue representatives, and constituency-oriented members described as local-issue members. Given the limitations of any one label, the policy versus constituency distinction is chosen as the most appropriate for this study although the issue versus local distinction is used as well.

Table 5.1 shows greater stability in the relative strength of these factions over time, far different than the pattern for the policy factions. Stalwarts and Provincials retain as much relative influence in the 103rd Congress as in the 97th Congress, although Stalwarts declined as a

TABLE 5.1
Constituency Factions in Each Congress
(Percentage of Conference)

	Congress						
	97th	98th	99th	100th	101st	102nd	103rd
Stalwart	35.9	30.5	23.3	25.4	25.7	28.9	35.8
Provincial	10.4	10.8	11.1	11.9	10.3	13.9	9.1
Placeholder	17.2	7.2	7.8	6.2	8.0	6.6	6.8

proportion of the conference in the middle years of the era. Placehold-ers, the most liberal constituency faction, experienced a strong decline similar to the liberal Patrician activists. Still, Placeholders number about 7 percent of the conference.

The geographic distribution of the constituency-oriented factions is also important, and illustrated in table 5.2, using data from the pivotal 101st Congress.

While these data will be discussed in greater detail for each faction, they show revealing patterns. First, the Stalwarts are distributed across the nation roughly similar to their representation in the whole House. The exceptions are the Mid-Atlantic, which is underrepre-sented in the Stalwart faction, and the Midwest which is overrepresen-ted. Provincials are almost exclusively in the contiguous Midwest, Border, and Mid-Atlantic regions, areas of traditional pragmatic, con-servative, and local-oriented Republicanism. Placeholders, the more liberal constituency-oriented group, is centered in the Mid-Atlantic states, which combine moderate national politics with a concern over local economies and regional industries.

Data on the voting patterns of all factions and their members were also collected in this study. These results are shown in table 5.3. Even

TABLE 5.2
Geographic Distribution of Constituency Factions
(Percentage of Faction in Region)

	New England	Middle Atlantic	Border States	Mid-West	South	Plains/ Rockies	Pacific
Stalwart	4.4	6.7	6.7	35.6	22.2	15.6	8.9
Provincial	0.0	16.7	27.8	33.3	11.1	0.0	11.1
Placeholder	7.1	57.1	0.0	14.3	0.0	7.1	14.3
Average	5.7	17.1	8.0	22.3	20.0	12.6	14.3

TABLE 5.3
Constituency Faction Voting Data Scores

	NJ Economic	NJ Social	NJ Foreign	NJ Mean	Fiscal Conserv.	NTU
Stalwart	16.71	20.66	19.71	19.03	1.38	80.88
Provincial	26.86	21.61	15.03	21.17	0.76	56.98
Placeholder	37.89	39.00	31.93	36.27	1.00	54.94
Average	20.33	23.38	20.13	21.28	1.25	73.56

among the constituency-oriented factions there is a wide divergence on general voting patterns, although it is not as large as that of policy factions. Generally, there is a relatively low fiscal-conservative ratio, which measures the relative conservatism on economic issues compared to other issues. Provincials especially, although virtually at the overall party mean, are spendthrifts on economic issues as measured both by the *National Journal* and the National Taxpayers Union.

Committee memberships, legislative and other activity levels, and caucus membership commitments were tabulated for each member in this study to examine different styles and patterns of behavior. The following three tables illustrate that data for constituency factions. Table 5.4 lists the standing committee memberships, table 5.5 the activity levels, and table 5.6 the caucus memberships.

As most of the data in the above tables indicate, these three factions are less interested in legislative activity and national policy and have less ideological voting patterns than the policy-oriented factions. They also tend to have lower overall committee and caucus membership levels, and these memberships are preponderantly in constituency-oriented groups. This analysis will discuss these constituency-oriented

TABLE 5.4
Constituency Faction Standing Committee Memberships

		Committee Type	
	Policy	Constituency	Influence
Stalwart	0.67	0.60	0.38
Provincial	0.44	0.72	0.44
Placeholder	0.21	0.93	0.29
Average	0.55	0.79	0.31

TABLE 5.5
Constituency Faction Activity Levels

	Party Committees	Legislative Activity	National Activity
Stalwart	1.91	0.87	4.91
Provincial	2.00	0.86	4.28
Placeholder	0.79	0.99	2.79
Average	1.97	1.00	5.23

TABLE 5.6
Constituency Faction Caucus Memberships

	Intraparty	National	Local	Total
Stalwart	0.71	1.24	1.04	3.00
Provincial	0.39	1.00	1.94	3.33
Placeholder	0.71	0.79	1.14	2.64
Average	0.85	1.58	1.42	3.85

members in two sections—the fiscally conservative and moderately active Stalwarts, and then the fiscally moderate and inactive Provincials and Placeholders.

Fiscally Conservative, Constituency-Oriented Group: Stalwarts

Stalwarts are the constituency-oriented faction with the lowest *National Journal* mean scores. The 101st House Republican Conference included forty-five Stalwarts, the largest number in any faction. Across the years included in this study, the faction has remained large and fairly stable, ranging from forty-two to sixty-nine members.

The label "Stalwart" suggests certain attitudes held by members of the faction. The label conveys a set of attitudes centered on preserving norms and fighting partisanship. Stalwarts are the protectors of party orthodoxy and tradition, the attitudinal and membership base for the older party leadership. Stalwarts attempt to combine the sometimes contradictory goals of support for the institution and party advancement, with different members emphasizing one objective over the other. These crosscutting pressures in the faction were at work in the

1989 Whip race, where twenty-three Stalwarts supported Madigan and twenty-one voted for Gingrich.

Stalwarts

Table 5.1 lists the relative numerical strength of the faction during the period in question. The Stalwart membership high point was in the 97th Congress of 1981–82 when it reached sixty-nine members and 36 percent of the conference. This rise is probably at least partly artificial given that this was the first congress of Reagan's first term, and House Republicans looked for legislative initiative to the new Republican president and the newly Republican Senate. The Stalwart proportion declined in the next few elections to consist of about 25 percent of the conference, and appears to be stabilizing at about 30 percent of House GOP members. The rise to 35 percent in the 103rd Congress can be discounted a bit because of the unusually high number of freshman Republicans in the class of 1992 and the tentative nature of first-term data. Since freshmen are likely to be very cautious in joining caucuses or voting against the party in their first years in the House, many first-termers may show up as Stalwarts when, in later congresses, their greater activism may push them into the Enterpriser or Moderate factions. For the 103rd Congress, in fact, twenty-two GOP freshmen were Stalwarts, a 50-percent-of-the-class mark not likely to be repeated after additional data are available.

The regional distribution of Stalwarts follows that of the GOP at large, with two important exceptions. There are fewer than the proportional number of Stalwarts in the Mid-Atlantic region, and more than the expected number of Stalwarts in the Midwest. Again, this might be expected of this older and more passive faction. Stalwarts would logically be more dominant in areas of traditional GOP strength rather than areas of new GOP growth in the South and Pacific. In addition, their conservative nature would lead one to expect fewer in the areas inhabited by moderate and liberal Republicans—the Northeast and Mid-Atlantic regions. So the Stalwart faction appears to be appropriately labeled as the core of the Republican old guard, a faction similar to the Stalwarts of A. James Reichley's analysis of the Nixon/Ford years.

The regional and electoral bases of Stalwarts seem representative of all Republicans in the House. In the 104th Congress, remaining Stalwarts included Carlos Moorhead of California, who was passed over for the chairmanships of the Commerce and Judiciary Committees for more active members; Bud Shuster of Pennsylvania, with a reputation as a pragmatic politician even though he is allowed to chair a committee in the 104th Congress; Jimmy Quillen of Tennessee, the senior member but not chairman of House Rules; Floridians like Clay Shaw and Bill Young; and Ohioans like David Hobson and Mike Oxley. Stalwarts who had left the House before GOP majority status include such rock-ribbed Republicans as Republican Leader Bob Michel, Bill Broomfield of Michigan, Clarence Miller of Ohio, James Broyhill of North Carolina, and Manuel Lujan of New Mexico. Most of these members are not or were not well-known outside the halls of Congress. Inside, however, their behavior was a distinguished mix of party loyalty to Republicans and loyal opposition to Democrats. They were the loyal "war horses" of the Reagan-Bush era, faithfully promoting Republican presidential initiatives despite personal misgivings or regional concerns they might have held. Stalwarts were often ranking committee or key subcommittee members, obtaining choice assignments through patient accumulation of seniority and accommodation of interests expressed by fellow members of the old guard.

The Stalwart voting scores and ratios as illustrated in table 5.3 also indicate the centrist policy nature of the faction. The individual *NJ* scores are consistently two to three points below the House GOP means, putting the group slightly to the right of the GOP center. In addition, the Stalwart fiscal conservatism ratio of 1.38 is virtually identical to the party's 1.37. The Stalwart voting profile mirrors the pragmatic, positional conservatism practiced by the leadership and most of the House GOP rank and file during the 1980s, and which was finally upset with the ascension of Gingrich to elected leadership.

The voting scores displayed in the table suggest that Stalwarts are consistently conservative. The data on standing committee memberships show the relative clout of the Stalwart faction during most of the period studied. Stalwarts averaged 0.67 policy committee positions per member, the highest of any faction and close to the Enterpriser and Patrician policy-oriented groups. The Stalwarts averaged fewer constituency committee memberships than the mean, with the faction averaging 0.6 and the GOP as a whole 0.79. Finally, the Stalwart score for influence committees was significantly above the mean of 0.31 at 0.38.

Activity-level data reaffirm that Stalwarts are at the center of the old party. All these measures for Stalwarts are below the GOP mean. Their legislative activity level is quite low at 0.87, and their national activity and party committee activity levels are also below the GOP mean. Their caucus activity level is also low, nearly the lowest of all factions for all types of caucuses.

Because of their fairly high level of membership on policy and influence committees, Stalwarts probably have a natural interest in obtaining influence within the House. In fact, as House partisanship increased in the latter post-reform era the Stalwarts were probably the least affected faction. Majority Democrats still had to consult with the Republican Leader on at least a few procedural items, and Speakers O'Neill and Foley, at least, maintained fairly cordial personal relations with Michel. Committee chairmen also often consulted with a few Stalwarts on their committees because of decades of personal friendship and individual courtesy.

The data also point out how appropriate are the implications of the Stalwart label. This faction is the most loyal to the party and to the institution. It included most House leaders in most of the Reagan-Bush era, even though its issue positions are right of the party mean. This tendency of congressional leadership to be more ideologically "pure" is, in fact, typical of all four congressional party caucuses, and particularly of the two party caucuses in the House.[1]

Because of their desire for and relative success in keeping influence within the Democratic House, the "good soldiers" in the Stalwart faction were unlikely to want to develop a highly confrontational House Republican agenda that challenged too strongly either a Democratic House majority or a Republican president. Stalwarts were always still able to make deals, even at the height of partisanship. Pat Roberts on the Agriculture Committee could count on mutual accommodation in meeting the needs of his Kansas farm constituency. Bud Shuster could work closely with Public Works Committee Chairman Robert Roe to ensure continued funding of Pennsylvania roads. Carlos Moorhead was a usually harmless and sometimes helpful adversary for legislative masters John Dingell and Henry Waxman on the Energy and Commerce Committee. Bill Dickinson could faithfully push Republican defense policy but still, in the final analysis, vote for the Armed Services Committee bill. Manuel Lujan would lose quietly on the Science or Interior Committees, going through the motions of partisan opposition while accepting the inevitability of Democratic hegemony. Bill Broomfield would work diligently for *contra* aid or additional foreign military assistance, but after losing quietly go back into the shadows of the Foreign Affairs Committee. Stalwarts were the least likely, for practical and attitudinal reasons, to "rock the boat" in a Democratic Congress.

Fiscally Moderate, Constituency-Oriented Groups: Provincials and Placeholders

Provincials and Placeholders are the last organized factions. Provincials have a mean *National Journal* score higher than Stalwarts and approximately at the GOP mean, while Placeholders' mean score is quite far above the Republican average. Provincials have the lowest legislative activity level of any faction, while Placeholders have extremely low activity levels across the other areas measured. Placeholders are quite a bit like their more conservative cousins, the Provincials, and could reasonably be labeled as moderate Provincials. But their significant inactivity in most policy areas justifies Placeholder identification as a separate group within the House GOP.

The term "Provincial" implies an attention to local issues. Provincials focus their representational efforts on distributional matters like particular items in appropriations bills and special public works authorizations. Based on these characteristics, Provincials could be expected to be strongly opposed to the Gingrich candidacy in the 1989 Whip race. That indeed was the case, as Gingrich received only six of eighteen Provincial votes.

The term "Placeholder" suggests low levels of activity. Placeholders might likely see their time in the House as temporary, either as an obligation or as a way station to another position. Both perspectives on their jobs would tend to limit Washington activity. Alternatively, Placeholders might find themselves closed out of significant congressional activities because of their liberal voting differences with the party leadership. "Placeholder" can also suggest passivity in attitudes toward congressional partisanship and party feeling, unwilling or unable to confront directly the Democratic majority and its perceived abuses.

Provincials

Table 5.1 lists the percentage of Provincials in each of the relevant congresses. That data indicate that the number of Provincials produced by the model varied little over the period, ranging only from sixteen to twenty-three, and averaging about nineteen. There was remarkably little "bounce" among the congresses. The geographical dispersion of Provincials is also narrow, as about two-thirds of the group hails from the Border states or the Midwest, with the remainder scattered among the South, Mid-Atlantic, and Pacific. No Provincials were found in either New England or the Plains/Rockies, the respective homes of moderates and economic conservatives. The Provincial faction is also the most rural faction in the House, this despite its lack of representation in the rural Plains/Rockies. The rural nature of this faction may further explain the voting pattern, reflecting the motivation to provide public works, agriculture or other spending programs to rural, poor constituencies. Provincials are concentrated in rural areas with traditional Republican roots—upstate New York, the Midwest, and a few Border states. Conversely, there are no Provincials from either New England or the Plains, the centers of policy-oriented Republicanism.

The list of Provincial members in the 104th Congress includes, not surprisingly, several senior members of the House Appropriations Committee, including senior Republican Joseph McDade of Pennsylvania, John Myers of Indiana, Ralph Regula of Ohio, Harold Rogers of Kentucky, Frank Wolf of Virginia, Joe Skeen of New Mexico, and Jerry Lewis of California. Other Provincials not on Appropriations include Don Young of Alaska, Steven Schiff of New Mexico, Paul Gillmor of Ohio, and Curt Weldon of Pennsylvania. All these Provincial members, those on the Appropriations Committee and those off it, have reputations as being immensely concerned with local, constituent-oriented issues. Regula is a strong supporter of the domestic steel industry because of its importance to his district. Weldon has probably been the most creative Provincial, creating a Congressional Fire Caucus to take advantage of the well-organized volunteer and professional fire departments in his Philadelphia-area district. With rare exceptions, Provincials do not involve themselves in major, creative national policy initiatives but are likely to pay close attention to the folks back home. As such, they are the faction most unlike the current House Enterpriser and Moralist leadership.

Provincial members of Congress who left before the Republicans took the majority include members of similar profile. Among these are Virginians Stan Parris and Bill Wampler, Norm Lent of New York, Robert Davis of Michigan, Ray McGrath and Guy Molinari of New York, Helen Bentley of Maryland, and, perhaps most significantly, Ed Madigan of Illinois. These Provinicials, too, showed more concern for local interests. Bentley gave up a reasonably secure House seat for an uphill governor's race, and Molinari quit the House for local office on

Staten Island. As one would expect of this faction, they voted strongly for Madigan in the 1989 House Whip race, giving their fellow faction member two-thirds of their eighteen votes.

Table 5.3 compares the texture of the Provincial record to the texture of the entire House Republican conference for the 101st Congress. While the Provincial mean *NJ* score of 21.17 is close to the party average, the variation on the specific scores is far greater. The Provincial economic score is about six points higher than the party average, indicating that Provincials are far more willing to spend federal dollars than are typical House Republicans. This impression is reinforced by the NTU score for Provincials, which at fifty-seven is far more spendthrift than the Moderate faction, and nearly as generous as the liberal Patricians. To make up for this relative liberalism on spending, the Provincial social and foreign policy scores are both more conservative than average. The typical Provincial social policy score is slightly, and the foreign policy score is significantly, more conservative than that of all Republicans. The voting pattern results in a fiscal conservative ratio of 0.76, far below any other faction. Consequently, the three dimensions of the Provincial vote indicates that faction members fit a "populist" profile of a strong military and conservative social values, but have a willingness to protect and promote federal programs that provide benefits to constituencies.

Table 5.4 displays the type of standing committee memberships of each faction. Provincial committee memberships reflect the same attention to constituency concerns as anticipated by the other data. The group is underrepresented on policy committees, about at the mean in constituency committees, and strongly overrepresented on influence committees. In fact, the Provincial influence committee membership average of 0.44 is the highest of any faction, even higher than that of the bedrock GOP Stalwarts. The focus of the Provincial interest is to obtain internal influence to achieve their localist goals. These data are further reinforced by the activity and caucus data provided in tables 5.5 and 5.6. Provincial legislative activity (a ratio measure based on bills sponsored and cosponsored) is the lowest of any faction, probably indicating their ability to work quiet legislative deals with majority Democratic committee chairmen while the GOP was in the minority. The national activity level is also quite low, and party activity at just about the GOP mean.

The caucus data further reinforce this general impression. Provincials are the least likely of any faction to be involved in intraparty caucuses in either the right or the left wings of the congressional party, and far less likely to be members of national-issue caucuses. On the other hand, members of this faction are the most likely of any Republican group to be part of local, narrow interest caucuses, with their 1.94 average far above the GOP mean of 1.42.

Provincials supported the old norms and took part in the traditional legislative process, even within the increasingly hostile partisanship of the 1980s and early 1990s. The Provincials' relative economic liberalism is also faintly reminiscent of the New Deal issue consensus of a strong military, traditional values, and generous social spending. Indeed, the contour of the Provincial voting profile as more liberal on economic issues than other issues is similar to the contour of most Democrats, but unique to the GOP. The high amount of Provincial legislative activity in combination with this voting profile indicates that a fair amount of cooperation with Democrats occurred during most of the post-reform era.

The overall picture of the Provincial faction that this analysis provides is significantly different from the pictures of policy-oriented factions. First, the faction's voting contour is vastly different. By any measure, Provincials are more liberal on economic issues than on other issues, a pattern the opposite of all policy-oriented factions. Activity measures, which estimate attitudes toward norms and issues, also make clear distinctions. The low fiscal conservatism suggests strong Provincial assent to a pragmatic approach.

These impressions are validated in the biographies of several Provincials. John Paul Hammerschmidt, despite his support for Gingrich in the Whip race, was known mostly for the local benefits he procured in his senior positions on the Public Works and Transportation, and Veterans Affairs, Committees.[2] John Myers of Indiana is fond of describing the energy and water appropriations bill, which originates from the subcommittee on which he served as ranking member, as an "All-American bill" that touches "every congressional district in our country directly." In fact, Myers once threatened other Republicans with lost projects if they opposed the energy and water or other appropriations bills on the House floor.[3] Joe McDade, as another senior member of the House Appropriations Committee, is also known for tapping that position for benefits for his district and those of his colleagues.

Many other Provincials are noted for being conservative on most issues, except in a narrow area where their local constituency is concerned. For example, Helen Bentley made a name for herself by bashing—sometimes literally—Japanese products, a popular position in her blue-collar Baltimore district.

Placeholders

Placeholders are a fast-dwindling share of the House GOP, as the data in table 5.1 show. They were the second largest faction in the 97th Congress of 1981–82, with thirty-three members accounting for 17 percent of the Conference. Their numbers fell to twelve and their percentage to 7 in the 98th Congress (ten were not reelected in 1982), and have remained fairly stable at that level since.

The regional distribution of Placeholders in the 101st Congress is what one would expect from a moderately liberal, constituency-oriented Republican group. More than half are from the three Mid-Atlantic states, and the remainder are scattered across all regions except the conservative states of the South and Border regions. No Placeholder in the 101st Congress came from the Border states or South, the areas of greatest House Republican growth in the 1980s. While most Placeholders left the House before 1994, the few remaining in the 104th Congress included Wayne Gilchrest of Maryland, Bob Franks of New Jersey, Jim Greenwood of Pennsylvania, Rick Lazio of New York, and Scott Klug of Wisconsin. Placeholders who dropped from the House rolls before 1994 included Pennsylvanians James Coyne, Charles Dougherty, Marc Marks, and Eugene Atkinson; Ohioans Ed Weber and Lyle Williams; and David Emery of Maine; Joel Deckard of Indiana; and Tom Evans of Delaware.

The general characteristics of the Placeholder faction would lead one to believe that its members would strongly oppose the aggressive conservative partisanship of Newt Gingrich. Indeed, only two of the fourteen Placeholders in the 101st Congress supported the man from Georgia.

As shown in table 5.3, the voting pattern of Placeholders is fairly uniform over the *National Journal* issue areas, averaging in the thirty percentiles, and ranging from fifteen to seventeen percentage points above the House GOP average.

The committee membership scores in table 5.4 provide evidence for the assumption that Placeholders are tightly focused on local issues. The pattern suggests a faction, much like the Provincials but with less intensity, interested in obtaining a fair amount of internal influence in order to achieve limited, pragmatic goals to aid its own reelection prospects.

The activity data displayed in table 5.5 reinforce this impression. Placeholder legislative activity is just below the GOP average, somewhat higher than that of the other two constituency-oriented factions. But their national activity and party committee membership data fall far below the GOP mean, and both far below the nearest other faction. For example, the Placeholder party committee activity score of 0.79 is just over half that of the next lowest faction, the Moralists, at 1.36. Caucus activity data is similar. One might expect a moderate group like Placeholders to have high intraparty caucus memberships, but the faction score is a low 0.71 compared to the GOP mean of 0.85. This is a higher score than that of Provincials, but identical to the centrist Stalwarts, and far below the policy-oriented Moderate score of 1.25. National caucus memberships are the lowest of all factions, and even local caucus memberships are low, only slightly above those of the more electorally secure Stalwarts.

These measures allow us to draw several conclusions. First, most of the faction's scores are significantly more liberal than the conference mean, putting Placeholders on the left side of the party with the Moderates, in the wide space between Stalwarts/Provincials and Patricians. Second, the Placeholder pattern of voting (about thirty-three on the *National Journal* scale) hinges between conservatism and moderation in the overall House. All measures indicate that the faction is rather passive, a group comfortable with old congressional norms. Low activity in almost every area leads one to question their motivations. It also makes more difficult an assessment of the group. Placeholders seem to ask little of Congress for their districts, and appear to be uninterested in ideological battles for party supremacy. A major problem in getting this faction to stand out is its very passivity.

A few things seem clear, however. Generally, Placeholders are considered by their fellow House Republicans to be at the liberal end, so in general they carry little weight within the House GOP. There are, however, a few exceptions. These few members started their careers earlier, were closer to the then-mainstream of the House GOP, and were more influential in its ranks. For example, Carl Pursell of Michigan was active on legislation and influential in policy decisions, and there are other examples such as McDade and Jim Courter of New Jersey.

Younger and more junior Placeholders, however, seem to have to fight a climate of suspicion about them and their loyalty to the party and its new, narrower social and foreign policy agenda. Given the overall House Republican trends—the geographic trend toward greater southern and western representation and the ideological trend toward social and foreign policy conservatism—Placeholder influence will probably further decline even if their numbers hold steady.

Summary

The various data sources in this chapter and the previous chapter work reasonably well in segregating House Republicans and placing like-minded members in factions. Several measures reinforce one another. For example, the voting texture across three issue areas, the three different types of standing committees, and the caucus participation divided into three different groups tended to coincide. The voting measures tended to identify those who were more sensitive to domestic economic issues by relatively more liberal *NJ* economic and NTU scores. Most often, these members would have higher participation in constituency-oriented standing committees and regional and industry-based caucuses. Second, the data, in some cases rather surprisingly, tended to divide members in factions that each had strong regional bases. This was especially true for Patricians centered in New England and the Mid-Atlantic, but it was also true for many other factions such as the Placeholders in the Mid-Atlantic. Third, the impression that most Republicans are alike was shown to be untrue. Unidimensional analysis places most House Republicans in the conservative one-third of the House, with large clusters of members right at, or slightly more conservative than, the party mean. The more detailed analysis presented here makes more distinctions.

The purpose of this analysis—to describe reasonably cohesive House GOP groups with stable patterns of voting and activity (not to identify specific individuals as "locked into" particular factions that could not change)—was met. The different sizes and characteristics of each faction could be described in that context, and the information could be transferred to congresses before and after the key 101st Congress and the defining Whip race of March 1989. Of course, many individual members moved to other factions. In addition, younger factions strengthened and older factions dwindled. The seven factions identified here, however, are based on behavioral and personal interest distinctions among members that have strong justification from earlier studies of Congress. It seems likely, then, that these factions will remain in the future and help explain House Republican activity and conflict in their new majority status.

Notes

1. Barbara Hinckley, "Congressional Leadership Selection and Support: A Comparative Analysis," *Journal of Politics* 32 (1970): 268–87; and Aage R. Clausen and Clyde Wilcox, "Policy Partisanship In Legislative Leadership Recruitment and Behavior," *Legislative Studies Quarterly* 12 (1987): 243–63.
2. Phil Duncan, ed., *Congressional Quarterly's Politics in America 1990: the 101st Congress* (Washington, D.C.: Congressional Quarterly, 1989), 81–83.
3. Duncan, *Politics 1990*, 508.

Chapter 6

House Republicans: From "Permanent" Minority to Pugnacious Majority

The contemporary House Republican Conference is divided into several factions. Not all important divisions divide neatly along voting lines. Equally critical divisions are over attitudes about congressional norms, bipartisanship, and representational styles.

This final chapter puts this description of House Republican factions into a broader historical and political context. It first describes some factional changes in the House Republican conference from 1980 to its ascension to majority status in 1995. It then examines the 1992–95 period of heightened activity in aggressively seeking, and then securing, majority congressional status. It concludes by speculating about the future of the House Republicans.

Secular Changes Within the House Republican Party in the Reagan-Bush Era

Many studies of congressional party changes include a review of party geographical shifts. Tables 6.1 documents this frequently cited information for the House Republican Conference, in percentage terms, from the 97th Congress through the 104th.

The South is the one region with clear relative gains in the House GOP conference. This gain is mirrored almost perfectly by the combined losses from the Midwest, Mid-Atlantic, and Border regions. On the other hand, the regions of New England, the Plains/Rockies and the Pacific retained almost exactly the same proportional influence in the decade and one-half studied here.

133

The strongest message of table 6.1 is the secular growth in the strength of southern House Republicans. This growth in relative regional strength occurred in both good and bad election years, with southern gains in the generally favorable 1984, 1992, and 1994 elections as well as in the disappointing 1982 and 1990 contests. This growth moved the South from a region that had about one-half the representation of the Midwest in 1980 to one larger than the Midwest as the end of minority Republican status approached.

This gross measure provides some information about changing relative regional strength. The shift from the Mid-Atlantic, Border, and Midwest to the South is the largest regional shift within the party. Regional balance in the House Republican leadership may have been a factor electing southerner Gingrich over midwesterner Madigan in the 1989 Whip race, but regional change is of more lasting importance for what it says about the internal factional composition of the House Republican party, and is made clearer by a discussion of factional shifts.[1]

The voting scores used in this analysis also provide some information about the dynamics of change. Table 6.2 displays the mean *National Journal* scores within the House Republican Conference for each of the Congresses from the 97th through the 103rd. The scores in the table are the mean of all individual mean scores for all GOP members in a particular Congress. The information in table 6.2 displays some evidence to support the argument that major ideological changes have taken place within the congressional party in this era.

TABLE 6.1
Regional GOP Representation: 97th–104th Congresses
(Percentage of Republican Conference)

	New England	Middle Atlantic	Border States	Mid-West	South	Plains/ Rockies	Pacific
97th	4.7	19.8	9.9	26.6	15.1	10.9	13.0
98th	4.8	17.4	7.8	25.2	17.4	13.8	13.8
99th	5.6	16.7	7.8	22.8	16.7	13.3	13.3
100th	5.1	17.5	7.9	23.2	17.5	13.0	14.1
101st	4.6	17.3	8.1	22.5	17.3	12.7	14.5
102nd	3.6	18.7	7.2	22.3	18.7	12.1	14.5
103rd	4.6	17.1	7.4	21.0	17.1	10.8	14.2
104th	3.5	13.8	6.0	22.4	26.3	12.9	15.1

TABLE 6.2
House GOP *NJ* Voting Measures, 97th–103rd Congresses

	Mean	Economic	Social	Foreign
97th(1981–82)	29.11	22.92	30.84	33.56
98th(1983–84)	21.12	19.49	22.70	21.19
99th(1985–86)	21.05	21.54	21.71	19.90
100th(1987–88)	20.28	19.69	22.19	18.95
101st(1989–90)	21.28	20.33	23.38	20.13
102nd(1991–92)	18.98	18.21	19.83	18.90
103rd(1993–94)	18.61	16.77	20.71	18.33

The *National Journal* voting scores are, of course, relative measures in which conservatism and liberalism are measured not against a fixed standard but only among the pool of members in a particular Congress. As such, to the extent that the entire Congress became more conservative in the post-reform era, a shift toward more conservative scores for House Republicans would mean that the shift within the party was even more pronounced than for the Congress as a whole. Conversely, if the entire Congress shifted to the ideological left, the greater conservatism within the GOP would be overstated. Studies examining this point reach different conclusions about the ideological drift of the House, but all find a greater homogenization of the House Democratic party because there are fewer conservative, usually southern, Democratic House members. It is likely that the House drifted "left" in the post-reform era while the House GOP drifted "right," but this question of absolute change is outside the scope of this study.

In any case, it can be stated with confidence that between the 97th and 103rd Congresses the House Republican Conference has become much more conservative. The largest jump came in the 1982 elections, where the *NJ* mean dropped eight points. Two factors, one geographical and the other internal to the House, account for the shift. Geographically, most Republican losses in 1982 were in the more moderate GOP regions of the Mid-Atlantic and Midwest, and the voting score change partially reflects the fact that regional members with moderate voting records did not return to the 98th Congress. The shift toward conservatism extends to all three *NJ* issue areas, but the change is far more prominent in foreign and social policy than in economic policy, where it was already quite low. Internally, after 1982 House Democrats lost their fear of an imminent GOP takeover of the House. As the data in earlier chapters showed, the increased partisan use of rules, procedures, and informal leadership mechanisms began to rise at the onset of the 98th Congress in 1983. In a real sense, 1983 marks the beginning of the hostile environment that was to consume the House in this era and eventually lead to united Republican aggression and ultimate Democratic failure.

Of additional interest is the second conservative dip beginning with the 102nd Congress of 1991–92. Two critical things occurred in the 101st Congress that probably led to this additional move to conservatism. First, of course, was the Gingrich victory over Madigan in the 1989 Whip race, soon after the beginning of the 101st Congress. With this event, aggressive conservatives openly hostile to the "go along, get along" style of the old House GOP leadership held their first formal leadership place near the top of the ladder.[2] Formal power began to be exercised by Gingrich and his cohorts, cutting into the previous virtual hegemony of power the old guard held. The second event of the 101st Congress was President Bush breaking his "no new taxes" pledge during the summer and fall fiscal year 1991 budget negotiations. The timing of the pledge's abandonment, just before an off-year election, was incredibly bad from a partisan perspective, irrespective of its wisdom as fiscal policy. The episode cut the president's credibility with House Republicans, and the poor 1990 election results advanced the standing of strong antitax critics such as Dick Armey of Texas.

As a whole, the table suggests two waves of ideological change in the era. The first wave is a general conservatism benefitting from the "purification" of the 1982 election losses, stabilizing at about that level for the remainder of the 1980s. The second wave is a resurgent economic conservatism expressed in a deepening aversion to tax increases, originating in the aftermath of the 1990 budget summit and off-year elections.

Shifting House Republican Factions: 1980 to 1995

While the above data are useful, the changing dynamics of the House Republican party are best illustrated by observing the changing relative size of the factions identified by this analysis. Table 6.3 displays the percentage power of the factions during this period. It sheds much light on factional shifts and reinforces the impressions created by the geographical and voting changes just noted.

The activist, conservative Enterprisers and Moralists dramatically

TABLE 6.3
Factions in Each Congress
(Percentage of Conference)

				Congress			
	97th	98th	99th	100th	101st	102nd	103rd
Moralist	7.3	15.0	21.7	14.7	18.9	22.3	21.6
Enterpriser	9.4	21.6	18.9	24.9	19.4	16.3	14.8
Stalwart	35.9	30.5	23.3	25.4	25.7	28.9	35.8
Provincial	10.4	10.8	11.1	11.9	10.3	13.9	9.1
Placeholder	17.2	7.2	7.8	6.2	8.0	6.7	6.8
Moderate	5.7	9.0	10.6	11.3	11.4	9.0	10.8
Patrician	14.1	6.0	6.7	5.7	6.3	3.0	1.1

raised their percentages during the period, especially after the 1982 elections. For the next portion of the Reagan-Bush era, the Enterpriser faction appeared to be larger than the Moralist faction. Since about 1990, however, (perhaps not coincidentally with the emergence of the Christian Coalition as a viable organization), the Moralist faction appears to be growing and overtaking Enterprisers as the largest activist, conservative group. Whereas only 7 percent of Republicans in the 97th Congress were Moralists, by the 103rd Congress the faction tripled. Enterprisers are close behind, as their percentage approximately doubled in the era. Together, these two factions grew from one-sixth of the House GOP Conference to more than one-third. Moderates also grew in influence during the era, growing from under 6 percent of the conference in 1981 to nearly 11 percent in 1994.

On the losing end of the ledger were Placeholders and Patricians. Placeholders fell from a faction equal in size to the Moralists and Enterprisers combined in 1981, to a group with under 7 percent of the conference in 1994. Patricians also declined severely, losing half their clout right after 1982 and declining steadily to near extinction by 1994. As mentioned previously, many of the 1981–82 Patricians who remained in Congress started to vote more conservatively or act more passively, behaviors that place them in the Moderate or Placeholder factions in later congresses.

This study has grouped the factions into constituency-oriented and policy-oriented dispositions, and divided each of these categories into factions of different ideological views. Examined from this perspective, the fates of the constituency-oriented groups have stayed fairly

stable while the fates of policy-oriented groups have diverged significantly.

The policy implications of the factional shifts are seen in table 6.4,
which pairs together the seven factions into the four groups that
organized the discussion of factions in this analysis—policy-oriented
conservatives, constituency-oriented conservatives, policy-oriented
moderates and constituency-oriented moderates.

The bottom portion of table 6.4 contains information about the two
separate shifts that occurred among House Republicans; the first shift
on the conservative/moderate ideological spectrum and the second
change on the policy/constituency behavioral scale.

If only the change in ideology is considered, the proportion of House
Republicans holding to a conservative line increased relatively little
and only at one point. Most of the change occurred after the 1982
elections with the major losses in the Mid-Atlantic region. After that
time, the proportion of members in the conservative factions changed
little. Similarly, if only the policy activism of members is considered—
without regard to ideology—activism grows from just under 40 percent
to just below 50 percent. Again, the number of members in policy-
oriented factions jumped most after the 1982 elections, and actually
fell slightly after that. As such, the rise in general activism is also clear
but not particularly sharp.

TABLE 6.4
House GOP Factional Changes, 97th–103rd Congresses
(Percentage of Conference)

				Congress			
	97th	**98th**	**99th**	**100th**	**101st**	**102nd**	**103rd**
Policy							
Conservatives	16.7	36.5	40.6	39.6	38.3	38.6	36.4
Constituency							
Conservatives	35.9	30.5	23.3	25.4	25.7	28.9	35.8
Policy							
Moderates	19.8	15.0	17.2	17.0	17.7	12.0	11.9
Constituency							
Moderates	27.6	18.0	18.9	18.1	18.3	20.5	15.9
TOTALS							
Policy	36.5	51.5	57.8	56.6	56.0	50.6	48.3
Conservative	52.6	67.0	63.9	65.0	64.0	67.5	72.2

When the twofold classification of voting together with activity is used, two major changes become apparent. The first is a conservative surge in policy advocacy as seen in the rise of Moralists and Enterprisers. The second was the parallel fall of the party's most liberal policy-oriented members, as seen by the almost total obliteration of the Patrician faction.

These shifts are clearly illustrated in noting the shifting percentages of policy-oriented moderates (Patricians and Moderates) and policy-oriented conservatives (Moralists and Enterprisers). In the 97th Congress of 1981–82, policy interest within the House Republican party was dominated by moderates who, although they comprised only about one-fifth of the conference, outnumbered policy-oriented conservatives about four to three. Twelve years later, the relative strengths were drastically different. Policy-oriented conservatives were about 35 percent of the conference and, more important for policy issues, held a three-to-one proportional advantage over policy-oriented moderates.

In 1981, conservatives were overwhelmingly constituency-oriented, as more than twice as many conservatives tended to local concerns as national policy matters. On the other hand, in 1981 about 40 percent of moderate Republicans were policy-oriented. By the end of the era, policy and constituency conservatives were at rough parity with each other, and conservative policy-oriented members numbered far more than moderate policy-oriented members.

House Republican policy-making in the early 1980s (and probably before) was dominated by moderate Republicans. At the end of the era, however, House Republican policymaking was dominated by conservatives. It was thus more ideological, activist, independent, and less sympathetic to traditional appeals to conventional norms.

The result is a far different House Republican party as it began its majority rule in 1995. Before 1980 the moderate, activist wing of the party worked with the majority Democratic leadership in crafting legislation and maintaining traditional norms. But policy interest moved to the conservative GOP wing at the same time partisanship overcame the House. Thus, the opportunities for bipartisan cooperation diminished for two reasons: GOP activism was far more conservative and ideologically distant from that of the Democrats, and the Democratic strategy was to shut off both GOP conservatives and moderates from policy cooperation. The combination of conservative activism and Democratic exclusion drove Republican activists of all stripes together.

All this time, there was little action within the constituency-oriented factions. They quietly maintained their standing within the party and in the House leadership, hiding from the controversies involving the policy-oriented factions and seeking peace with a few willing Democratic power brokers. This situation defined the *status quo* during the middle 1980s.

The election of Gingrich to the Whip position in 1989 changed all that. In essence, the activist policy-oriented factions coalesced around Gingrich to defeat the more passive constituency-oriented groups that supported Ed Madigan. Gingrich's victory was the first and most important intraparty victory for this coalition of activists, who were to have later successes in other leadership races and in deciding the strategy for the critical 1994 majority-gaining election.

The 1992 Elections and Subsequent Leadership Changes

The strategy pursued consistently by Gingrich is to develop a "responsible" congressional Republican party with an attractive domestic agenda. His push toward greater party responsibility accelerated in the 1992 election cycle in the wake of President Bush's defeat and a new class of forty-seven House Republicans. The growing agreement in the conference with this move toward responsibility is seen most clearly in the several GOP leadership races held at the beginning of the 103rd Congress, and in the post-election developments in House GOP leadership organization and strategy.

Several leadership slots were contested at the beginning of the 103rd Congress, some of them open seats and others with incumbents facing challengers. In every case, the moderate candidates lost out to more activist conservatives.[3] The most interesting race was for chair of the Republican conference, the number-three leadership post in the party. The position was held by Stalwart Jerry Lewis of California, who was being challenged by Enterpriser Dick Armey of Texas. In a very close race, Armey ousted Lewis by a narrow 88–84 margin.[4] Armey's challenge to Lewis was based mainly on the charge that Lewis was too cozy with the majority Democrats. Lewis had used his position as ranking minority member on the Legislative Branch Appropriations subcommittee to broker deals with the majority leadership and blunt minority party attacks on the operations of Congress.

In many ways, the Armey-Lewis conference race contained the same dynamics of the Gingrich-Madigan Whip race a few years earlier, although many of the strategic details of the campaign differed and more than one-third of the Republican conference was new since 1989. Most interpreters of the race saw it as a showdown between the younger generation of more ideological conservatives, generally favorable toward Armey, and the party's more traditional and pragmatic wing in which Lewis had risen.[5]

The freshman class apparently was a decisive factor, as an estimated thirty-five to forty newcomers supported the challenger. As this analysis would predict, freshmen interpreted the Armey victory as a victory for activism, not necessarily conservatism. John Linder of Georgia said the freshman class was "looking for activity."[6] "People are quick to pin a conservative label on us," said Deborah Pryce of Ohio. "I prefer the label activist."[7] More precisely, the conservative revolution in the House GOP had taken its most decisive step ten years earlier, in 1982, while the 1992 results affirmed the victory of activism among conservatives.

Armey himself interpreted his victory as endorsing his calls for the party to return to economic issues. He also wanted to cultivate talent in the younger and more aggressive members of the House GOP, and to establish in the Conference a newly energized intellectual attack on Democratic programs. "What we want to do is discover who our geniuses are and back them,"[8] Armey said. These themes essentially bolstered Gingrich's desire to help create a more responsible House Republican party with a more positive domestic economic agenda.

With both Gingrich and Armey now in the leadership, House Republicans instituted several new programs and strategies to formulate and communicate coordinated party themes. The first, and arguably easiest, programs installed were reactive tools to counter the newly united Democratic White House and House of Representatives. Responding to the daily partisan attempt at media management by the House Democrat's "message board," House Republicans created a "theme team" to hone their messages—usually negative salvos aimed at Clinton policy.[9] The Conference also started several new initiatives and publications to coordinate policy. For example, in early January a "rapid response team" was formed (in blatant imitation of a Clinton campaign tool) to provide almost immediate party commentary countering policy statements or initiatives of the Clinton administration.

On the more positive side of message development, the conference instituted a weekly facsimile newsletter, "Boarding Pass," sent out on Thursdays (the day many members return to their districts for weekend constituency work) outlining party themes to use during weekend public appearances in districts. Other new programs initiated by the leadership included nationwide town meetings on timely issues before Congress, lengthy issue briefs treating substantive issues from a Republican perspective, formal consulting on national and regional media contacts and op-ed pieces, and even coordinating information about bills fellow House Republicans introduced.[10]

A final area of leadership organizational change begun early in 1993 was in coordinating alternative policies across the spectrum. The goal was to develop policies not only in traditional Republican areas such as defense, economic growth, and budget reform, but in areas of traditional Democratic popular strength such as health care, welfare reform, and congressional reform. House GOP efforts in 1993 and 1994 to develop party-wide alternatives were abetted by the House Democratic leadership, which early in the 103rd Congress had settled on a legislative strategy that completely shut out Republicans, even the most liberal of the party members.[11] Thus, the challenge of the new almost entirely conservative House Republican leadership—to include enough moderate Republicans in the policy development apparatus so that they would not be alienated from the party and defect to the majority on important votes—was made far simpler by the continued and deepened partisan atmospherics.[12]

By late 1993 the takeover of hostility between the parties in the House was complete—Democrats would neither seek nor allow Republican participation from any member of the minority party. As a result Republicans, even and perhaps especially those on the left edge of the party, became willing to take large risks to wrest control of the House from the Democrats.

The 1994 Election Strategy and Its Implementation

The key 1994 election strategy, the "Contract With America," was the emerging House Republican Leadership's vehicle to bring together the hostility of the party's diverse activist factions: Moralists hostile to dominant social trends they saw as evil, Enterprisers hostile to dominant economic policy they saw as foolish, and Moderates (and a few Patricians) hostile to dominant congressional procedures and norms they saw as unfair. Activist leaders calculated that if all activist factions were on board with a unified agenda, the passivist groups would accept, or at least not interfere in, the attempt to nationalize the 1994 elections.

House Republicans prepared the 1994 election strategy in the fall of 1993 as House partisanship peaked. National strategy making for congressional elections was a rare idea for the House GOP. A form of it was attempted in 1982, but the "stay the course" message backfired in reminding many voters just how bad times were. But the national strategy became a certainty for 1994 as Gingrich was joined in the leadership in 1992 by Armey at the conference and Bill Paxon of New York at the House GOP campaign committee (NRCC), and as Stalwart Republican Leader Bob Michel announced he was retiring in 1994. The new leaders were attuned to strategic politics, and they believed that injecting national themes into House races could greatly increase their numbers, perhaps even enough for a majority.

There was a strong argument in support of this view. The last few decades' growth in congressional staff, the rise of the frank, and the changed nature of lawmaking have altered the decision making calculus of voters in House elections. All these changes tended to benefit Democrats, as these new leaders argued. Staff growth made members better able to manipulate the bureaucracy to help favored constituencies. Staff was disproportionally Democratic, sometimes with committee ratios of five to one or six to one. Democrats also tended to use the frank more frequently and use it to advance particularistic benefits. One examination of franked mail found that Democrats were more likely to encourage individuals to solicit help from representatives, to mention pork-barrel projects, and to emphasize the programs that redistributed income. Republicans, on the other hand, were more likely to emphasize macroeconomic issues like growth and jobs, and to make pledges to limit the influence of Washington over people's lives.[13]

Researchers come to similar conclusions. John Petrocik found, for example, that issues were of minimal importance in the 1988 congressional elections. Over 40 percent of voters surveyed had nothing at all to say about House candidates other than a mere like or dislike of the person, and about three-fourths of voters stated that there were no issues being discussed in House elections.[14]

Issueless House elections disadvantage Republicans, since polls usually identify the GOP as the party more people trust to solve more of the problems on the public agenda. According to the new House GOP leadership, Republicans failed at least partly because House elections tend not to be issue oriented. Another problem was that the best GOP issues—national defense and general prosperity—were less salient in House elections. Key objectives for the GOP were to make issues more important in the 1994 House elections, and to change to the party's advantage the understanding of issues that would predominate in the 1994 campaign.

The critical strategy was to unify all those factions that might balk at a unified issue-based strategy, especially the Moderates and Patricians most accustomed to cooperating with Democrats. The first step in unifying the policy activists was to operate a different type of annual conference in Salisbury, Maryland, in February 1994. While each House party holds annual retreats, these events usually are unproductive, with too much socializing and too little strategic planning. At Salisbury, however, House Republicans engaged in "bigger question" efforts common to competitive businesses but rare to political parties—identifying common principles or core beliefs, agreeing on a vision based on those beliefs, writing a mission statement to give content to the vision, and developing a strategy to accomplish the mission.

The principles that House Republicans identified as common to them all were "individual liberty, economic opportunity, limited government, personal responsibility, and security at home and abroad." Their common vision was to "Renew the American Dream by promoting individual liberty, economic opportunity and personal responsibility, through limited and effective government, high standards of performance and an America strong enough to defend all her citizens against violence at home or abroad." And the jointly developed mission statement read "As House Republicans we will work together to offer representative governance, and to communicate our vision of America through clearly defined themes, programs and legislative initiatives to earn us the honor of becoming the Majority party in 1995."[15]

The House Republicans' "Contract With America" was the key strategy to accomplish the Salisbury mission. Gingrich, Armey, and Paxon coordinated efforts to survey all incumbents and House GOP candidates for their issue priorities to be used in a public contract. In addition, a small "marketing" steering group was charged with developing the most attractive way to describe and promote the issues chosen.

The members' and candidates' key issue interests became the elements of the contract—constitutional amendments on a balanced federal budget and term limits for House and Senate members; and legislation on a line-item veto, tax cuts, crime, welfare, the family and economic stimulation.

The third step in the process was "test marketing" the legislative elements: their wording, order, format and presentation. The marketing steering group was charged to carry out this task during the summer. Targeting Perot voters, conservative Democrats, and ticket splitters, the group received help from several pollsters, including Frank Luntz, who had served as Ross Perot's 1992 presidential campaign pollster. Polls and focus groups tested various themes and descriptions of the contract elements, influencing its wording, order, and presentation to make the broadest appeal.[16]

Based upon these findings, the group decided to drop any reference to Republicans in the document since party labels did not test well. The group found that the most appealing element of the contract was its contractual nature—that House Republicans asked to be voted out of office if they failed to bring the ten contract items up for a House vote in the first hundred days of a Republican 104th Congress.

For the nationalization strategy to succeed, members and candidates had to overcome the "minority mentality" that accepted institutional norms and opposition party status. Obviously, one step to achieve this goal was to work with all the policy-oriented party members from anywhere on the issue voting spectrum in compiling the list of contract items. A buy-in by all the activists would induce the constituency-oriented members to acquiesce, if not actively join, in the party strategy.

An additional part of the strategy was to present evidence on the unfairness of the Democrats. To this end, Armey undertook a member and candidate education effort, culminating in a lengthy progressive/populist critique of the House that he and far more liberal Christopher Shays of Connecticut and Jennifer Dunn of Washington released. The report charged that forty years of Democratic control had created an "interest group state" inimical to the interests of the American people.[17] The paper's main purpose was to give Republicans and receptive media arguments about and examples of Democratic unfairness in operating the institution of the House. This point was difficult to convey, but essential to the GOP strategy of broadening its attack on Democratic rule from policy to procedure, an area most likely to attract political moderates and skeptical media.

Conservative think tanks helped. Key players included the Heritage Foundation, with ties to the neoconservatives, and the Cato Institute, a think tank with more libertarian credentials. Christian Coalition staff also helped to shape contract elements, especially the $500-per-child family tax credit. All these groups met with party and congressional staff to flesh out the details of bills and write actual legislative proposals.[18]

There were many controversies in finalizing contract elements. Some Enterpriser-like members thought the contract did not go far enough toward populism, and wanted such measures as national initiative and referenda. Others Moralist-like representatives thought the document was weak on social conservatism because it was silent on abortion, school prayer, and homosexuality. Still others from the Moderate camp thought the contract was too conservative in areas like welfare reform. And many members, mostly in the constituency-oriented factions, thought it was a strategic mistake to inject issues into the 1994 campaign given that Clinton's popularity and the public esteem of Congress were low. They argued the party should be satisfied with the modest gains likely from an election held under unified government with an unpopular president. These disputes continued behind the scenes until the day the contract was unveiled on the Capitol steps, and emerged in public through election day.[19]

Notwithstanding these criticisms, a September 27 event on the west front steps of the Capitol unveiled the contract and, in general terms at least, shaped the rest of the campaign. One hundred fifty incumbents and nearly 180 challengers assembled to promise a vote, if not necessarily passage, of the contract's ten bills. After quite favorable first-day coverage, Democratic attacks and media attention focused on the balanced budget plank (which promised one by 2002) and the severe cuts Democrats alleged it would mean to Social Security. Daily polls showed that these attacks were having an effect because the contract did not show how a balanced budget would be achieved.[20] It took more than a week to write and disseminate an effective response to this charge, and by that time the attack was gaining some ground. This obvious mistake caused even more GOP grumbling over the contract strategy, but it was too late to turn back.

The first few days were not entirely negative, however. The GOP accomplished a major objective when on October 4 Ross Perot endorsed a Republican House on "Larry King Live." In addition, Congress recessed in early October having failed to act upon most significant items on the Democratic agenda for domestic policy or congressional reform. Clinton had early in his term abandoned a middle-class tax cut as inconsistent with his primary goal of deficit reduction. A crime bill squeaked through, but only after Republicans successfully cast it as laden with pork. Health care had fallen by the wayside in early September, partly from delays in finishing the crime bill but mostly because of successful House GOP attacks on it as expanding government bureaucracies. Campaign reform died from bipartisan procrastination, and lobbying reform was killed by Senate Republicans. Thus, in early October Democrats left Washington virtually empty-handed in the campaign's last weeks, especially in regard to domestic and congressional reform issues, usually their strongest suits but now central elements of the House GOP contract.

Although House Republican leaders were privately still optimistic, the media perceived the contract strategy to be at best a wash until October 23, when the *Washington Post* reported on a "secret" Alice Rivlin memo illustrating various tax increases and spending changes the Clinton administration should consider in developing future economic policy.[21] The memo, while sensible from a policy sense, was a disaster of political timing, recalling nothing so much as Bush's 1990 abandonment of his "no new taxes" pledge. The memo gave Republicans an opening to accuse Democrats of scheming to raise taxes and cut the same popular programs Democrats alleged the contract threatened. Happily for Republicans, the last few weeks were a confusion of charges and countercharges over taxes, spending and budgets, with Democrats newly on the defensive from the Rivliñ memo.

The 1994 Election and Its Aftermath

On November 8, 1994, the GOP gained fifty-two House seats, obtaining a majority of 230 seats for the first GOP control of the House since 1953. Much of the post-election debate is on what mandate the elections carry. One argument, made mostly by House Republicans, is that the startling election results are a mandate for the contract's ten elements. An opposing argument, usually made by Democrats, is that the contract had little effect on the voting and thus no popular standing. Few voters (only about 35 percent) had even heard of the contract. The 1994 vote, in this view, was an expression of concern over the direction of the nation, with Democrats were merely a convenient scapegoat since they controlled Congress. Both arguments contain elements of truth. The contract did help Republicans to become the House majority, but there is no clear mandate for most items in the contract save their initial popularity when they are briefly described to respondents of public opinion polls.

That is not to say the contract was not the key to the GOP majority. It was. Its most important effect was to change the discourse among candidates. The contract started off the most intense campaign period, from late September to election day, on an issue orientation rather than an incumbent-personality orientation. GOP issues were chosen for their popularity and were consciously packaged in the most appealing manner. And they addressed the same range of issues Congress had just left undone. While the contract was not well known by the public, every candidate knew of it. It thus dominated the debate among the candidates and the media accounts of many House campaigns. Most Democrats, anxious about defending Clinton, seized upon assumed vulnerabilities. In the vast majority of cases, however, their arguments were not persuasive. For example, an overwhelming number of Americans believe balancing the budget can easily be done. The Democratic response kept more House races on the topic of Republican-framed issues rather than Democratic personalities or incumbent personal performance. The issue focus intensified with the failure of the Clinton agenda in Congress, expensive DNC and RNC ad campaigns, Clinton's nonstop campaigning, and the leaking of the Rivlin memo.

Thus, by both design and luck, Republicans made the 1994 off-year elections far more focused on issues framed in a way that finally gave them an advantage. In this environment, traditional Democratic appeals had less legitimacy and in some cases were seen as attempts to run from the Democratic party and presidential records.

The marginally lower attraction of personal appeals made a critical difference in many elections. As such, it is fair to say the House GOP victory was not a mandate for the specific provisions of the contract, but rather for the strategy of creating a popular identity and message through issues. In other words, the campaign results endorsed a responsible congressional party creating its own domestic issue agenda.

Changes and Challenges in the 104th Congress

Majority status holds both opportunities and perils for the new House Republican majority, situations that are seen more clearly if there is a full understanding of the factions that make up the party. Throughout the first 100 days these factions held together remarkably well with the ten contract items providing great discipline for all majority members. But soon after the convening of the 104th Congress, splits among the factions became clear, identifying the challenges the Enterpriser/ Moralist leadership faces in managing the complex House Republican

Conference. The challenges will be many as the new majority seeks many legislative and institutional changes.

Legislative Issues

The legislative changes became more difficult after the relatively easy House consideration of the contract. In terms of this study, the contract is best seen as a political document addressing the procedural hostility of the Moderates, the economic policy hostility of the Enterprisers, and the cultural and social hostility of the Moralists. The genius of the contract and the leaders behind it was that it, and they, channeled that widely varied hostility in a successful attack on the long-standing House Democratic majority.

The contract itself was largely an Enterpriser document whose procedural reforms strongly appealed to policy moderates. These two groups gained most during the first 100 days, with the Moderates benefitting in a proportion far greater than their numbers. The first-day reforms were nearly all procedural. The changes included reductions in committees, subcommittees, and the attendant staff; making private-sector regulatory and labor laws apply to Congress; opening up the deliberative process at the committee level; limiting committee and subcommittee chairmanships to six years to curb potential abuses by these key leaders; and limiting the potential for procedural abuse by pledging more open floor rules.[22] Many of these reforms were approved by overwhelming bipartisan majorities, and several had long been pushed by moderate Republicans. As such, the first-day reforms were a clear victory for the Moderate/Patrician factions and a strong early payoff for their support of the remaining contract items.

The remaining contract items had far greater participation from members that this analysis identifies as Enterprisers and Moralists. Tougher crime and welfare legislation, legal and regulatory reform, domestic spending cuts and budgetary changes like a balanced budget amendment and legislative line-item veto, and tax cuts and business incentives are all at root Enterpriser initiatives. The Moralist elements in the contract were diluted or obscured in the original document as economic matters (for example, the $500-per-child tax credit) to enhance the strategy's appeal to key swing Perot voters, who are somewhat libertarian in their political views. Thus, most of the remaining items were most clearly Enterpriser planks strongly supported by Moralists, but not at the core of the latter faction's agenda.

The post-contract agenda was more difficult, and here the majority's factions challenged the new leadership. Nowhere has this been clearer than in budgetary policy. While Moderates and Patricians happily join other factions in passing procedural reforms, there is little Moderate enthusiasm for combining large tax cuts with balancing the budget by 2002. They would much prefer meeting the stated goal with no tax cut, or perhaps even small and selected tax increases.[23]

The concern about going "too far, too fast" on budget cutting is not exclusively a Moderate and Patrician concern, but one also shared by constituency-oriented Placeholders and Provincials. Provincials especially hold critical spots in key committees targeted to carry heavy loads in balancing the budget by 2002. Many Provincials serve on the Appropriations Committee, and were being asked to make large spending cuts to achieve party goals. Other Provincials hold key positions on such constituency committees as Agriculture and Transportation and Infrastructure (formerly the Public Works Committee). The "aggies" will work hard to limit the changes in farm programs and manipulate programs to achieve budget savings without comprehensive programmatic reform. Members of Infrastructure will act similarly, seeking to remove transportation trust-fund accounts from the unified federal budget to avoid real reductions but still claim fealty to balanced federal budgets. The Provincials are generally conservative, but they clearly feel threatened by aggressive attempts to balance the federal budget and cut programs from which they and their constituents have benefitted for years.[24]

The wishes of these factions leave the leadership in a quandary. Pledged to procedural fairness, if the party holds to such a pledge on budget votes Moderates or Provincials are likely to win floor attempts to restore spending as nearly all Democrats would vote for such efforts. Breaking the pledge of procedural fairness would, on the other hand, open the party leadership to strong criticism from the Moderate faction, the other party, and the many academic and media observers of the House who acknowledged the procedural unfairness of the previous Democratic majority.

Beyond the budget debate, Moderates are most likely to cause the leadership difficulties on issues such as campaign reform, lobbying reform, and social issues such as school prayer, abortion, and homosexuality, where the Moderates will be facing off against the far larger Moralist faction. Moderates will seek to push "reform" legislation. While they will find some aid from younger, more conservative members on these issues, congressional reform is regarded with disdain by most of the older factions, especially the Stalwarts, Provincials, and

Placeholders. This resistance, combined with the natural tendency for the majority to believe in its own purity of motives, presents a real tension within the conference and a challenge to the Enterpriser/ Moralist leadership, which generally does not feel strongly about the issue.

Endorsing and getting floor votes on the remaining Moralist social agenda presents its share of difficulties. One obstacle is the less enthusiastic support for these initiatives by Enterprisers, who hold the top leadership positions. Many leaders will point out that Republicans obtained a majority in the House with a contract nearly devoid of social issues. Moralists may acknowledge the point, but they are unlikely to back down from their claims given that their faction is the largest single policy-oriented faction, growing in strength every election cycle. The strong resistance of Moderates and Patricians to the Moralist agenda is a major obstacle. They are unlikely to extend their support to controversial items in their view inappropriate for congressional consideration. A final obstacle is the uncertainty over how the constituency-oriented factions will respond. Many Stalwarts might side with the Moralists when the social issues come to a vote. Provincials and Placeholders, however, are unlikely to help push these items to the top of the party agenda, not caring much one way or the other about congressional consideration of these divisive matters.

Formal organization of these factions was already occurring in early 1995. Moderate members were planning strategy in weekly "Tuesday lunch bunch" meetings, generally thought to be headed by Moderates Nancy Johnson, Steve Gunderson, and Fred Upton.[25] The group caused some trouble throughout the budget debates of 1995, complaining the tax-cut portion of the balanced budget package was too big and cuts in declines in domestic spending growth too severe. Socially conservative House Republicans, many in the freshman class, were also organizing in order to ensure consideration of their favorite Moralist legislation in the 104th Congress.[26] And Provincials were using their clout in key influence committees to achieve budget cuts on paper but program preservation in practice.

The legislative agenda and strategy for the new leadership is far from clear. The critical choice facing the Enterpriser/Moralist leadership is whether to seek coalitions with the other activists, the Moderates, or with the other conservatives, the Provincials and Stalwarts. Enterpriser Gingrich seems clearly to prefer an activist coalition, a strategy that he has always pursued. The preference of the leadership as a group is not as clear. The most promising general path may be to bring up much of the Moralist agenda under rules open enough so that Moderates can have a fair shot at amending or defeating the initiatives obnoxious to them. But to be successful at defeating these proposals, the Moderates will need to engage in a vigorous bipartisanship not likely to develop easily or quickly under House Republican rule or Speaker Newt Gingrich. In addition, the aggressive freshman class and Moderates are jointly supportive of lobbying and congressional reform legislation. Action on these agenda items might be necessary as a payoff for Moderate support for budget balancing and a response to freshman fear of appearing "domesticated" by the glamour of Congress.

None of this guarantees success. If budget balancing were the only House Republican success, voters could rightly wonder whether the cuts were too deep and whether Congress exempted itself from reform. If the social agenda were voted on and Moderates were unsuccessful in stopping it, the party would be straying from its proven 1994 winning formula of emphasizing economic and procedural issues and add to its ultraconservative image. It would thus become vulnerable in 1996 to the charges of intolerance and exclusivity it so adroitly avoided in 1994.

Institutional Issues

The institutional changes brought by the Republican majority, because they occurred so quickly, were clear fairly early in the 104th Congress. First, the contract pledges to cut committee staff by one-third and reform and downsize the institutional support offices. Most of these changes were accomplished by early summer 1994, while additional reductions and privatization were largely accomplished in the 1996 legislative branch appropriations bill.[27] The institutional pledge of procedural fairness is less clearly fulfilled. Most of the contract items were considered under rules far less restrictive than common practice under Democratic rule, but these rules were far from open. Several rules put strict time limits on the consideration of bills. This theoretically allowed any amendments to be considered in that time, but actually it severely rationed time and, thus, amendments considered with time limits.[28] Later agenda items were considered under modified rules, most of them less restrictive than Democrats proposed, but still far from open.

Most important to the institutional understanding of the House is how the institution and the Office of the Speaker are changing under the Republicans. These changes are complex and are occurring simultaneously. The important new work of Ronald Peters on the Speakership is a helpful guide in sorting out the key issues.[29] Peters identifies several levels of political context in which the House and the Speaker operate, from the large political system to the individual characteristics of each Speaker. Peters approaches the Office of the Speakership in historical context, but his system is also a useful starting point in identifying some of the key changes from the post-reform Democratic House to the new House under Republican rule. First, as Peters notes, the House is set within a larger political system and policy agenda. The key elements, which can change over time, are the function of political parties, the structure and expectations of the presidency, and key constitutional questions such as the power of federalism or the shape of the separation of powers. The 1994 election and the new Republican House majority are affecting all elements.

The 1994 Republican strategy enhanced the power of the party system. While weak, atomistic parties dominated the last few decades of Congress, the 1994 contract strategy showed that parties can be more organized and active around policy questions than they had been in previous elections. As such, the contract strategy may to some extent reinvigorate issue-oriented elections and revive responsible party advocates.

The second element occurring in the 104th Congress is the attempt to rein in the president. Some elements of the contract are clearly intended to weaken the office and the executive branch, including limiting regulations, cutting federal programs, and abolishing federal agencies and departments. In this area, there is a clear move to limit the bureaucracy and, because the president controls it, the executive's reach. While the new Republican Congress began some efforts to hand the president greater powers in some areas—passing a line-item veto and examining repeal of the War Powers Act—these efforts bogged down as new House members thought twice about granting new power to a partisan opponent. At the same time, the Speaker (both the office and most obviously its inhabitant in the 104th Congress) has come to challenge the presidency in terms of legislative agenda setting and public appeal, with as much or more media attention now paid to Speaker Gingrich as to President Clinton.[30] The constant thread in these changes is a reduction in the size and scope of the federal government and an attempt to shift more power to the Congress.

The third changing element is a reinvigoration of federalism. Most of the legislative initiatives pursued by the new majority in Congress give states far greater authority, if not greater budgetary resources, to manage their affairs. As such, the new Congress intends that the power of the national government (and Congress as part of the national government) over state and local governments be relimited.

Peters identifies key institutional characteristics that help to classify House Speakerships. This analysis adds to his two items of institutionalization and turnover, additional items focusing on the locus and concentration of internal power, and the level and dynamics of internal partisanship. All these are different at the onset of a Republican House. First, recent Houses had moderate institutionalization and moderate turnover. High institutionalization and low turnover both tend to rein in the power of the Speaker, while the opposite tendencies strengthen the Speaker's power. With the influx of new members after the 1992 and 1994 elections, and the radical changes of the 104th Congress, the Republicans control a House of less institutionalization and more turnover. These characteristics enhance the potential, if not the actual, power of the Speaker.

Other changes also suggest greater Speaker power in the Republican House. First, the locus and concentration of power looks vastly different. One of the reforms instituted by the new Republican majority was to strengthen the Speaker's hand in committee selection.[31] The Speaker was allowed to name committee chairs, and these chairs, in turn, could name subcommittee chairs. Thus, while "subcommittee government" dominated much of the previous Democratic era, Republican changes have reversed the flow of legislative agenda setting power back to the Speaker. A second change in the 104th Congress is the abolition of legislative service organizations (LSOs), the most prominent and aggressive form of congressional caucus.[32] At the beginning of the 104th Congress, Republicans voted to abolish all LSOs and limit these challenges to the Speaker's legislative agenda setting power. This action is understandable because LSOs compete with formal leaders for power, but somewhat ironic given the initial use of intraparty and other caucuses by the new GOP leaders in their attaining influence in the House. Remaining in place, however, is much of the leadership apparatus, such as a large Whip organization, Speaker's task forces, and large leadership staffs to communicate with and control competing power sources.

The consequences of these changes are very significant. Peters described the Democratic House of the 1960s to the early 1990s as headed by a "democratic Speakership" which had to be constantly in touch with individual members and groups of any size or influence in order to maintain order and legislative action. The Speaker during this "democratic" period was a therapist, policy maker, and symbol. Minority Republicans might claim Democratic speakers were far more partisan and Democratic leadership far more bureaucratic, believing that "democracy" extended only to Democrats. As such, Republicans could reasonably see the post-reform era as "bureaucratic partisan" and not "democratic." Indeed, the large Democratic leadership apparatus was highly bureaucratic in order to maintain contact with and control over so many powerful House Democratic members and small groups. It is also true that the Speaker was severely constrained by factions and groups within the majority party.

Republicans, by making the changes outlined above, have taken several steps to make sure that their Speakership is not held hostage by intraparty groups or independent members. If the last years of the Democratic Congress had a Speakership caught in games of "bureaucratic partisanship," the new 104th Congress has a Speaker exercising "charismatic partisanship." In the early 104th Congress, Speaker Gingrich relied on the charisma of himself and the individual ability of others to achieve party and institutional goals. First, he promoted several junior members to key committee chairs, and selected many freshmen for exclusive committees such as Rules, Appropriations, and Ways and Means.[33] Second, he made extensive use of his power to appoint task forces to address issues of large and small consequence.[34] As a third piece of evidence supporting the charismatic characterization the Speaker chose several individuals to head up short-term projects, such as Jim Nussle to manage the transition and Vern Ehlers to bring the House "on-line" on the Internet.[35]

The Speaker has been so active in setting up these personally accountable informal groups that he appears to be setting up competing power centers to accomplish identical goals, apparently seeing which members can most effectively carry out his objectives.[36] Finally, the Speaker himself, even in the early days of the 104th Congress, deferred many of the details of running the House to Majority Leader Armey, describing the Speaker's role as the "chief executive officer," and Armey's as the "chief operating officer" of the House.[37] As such, this description of "charismatic partisanship" dominating the new 104th Congress is a suitable summary of the Speaker's actions in the early portion of the 104th Congress.

The combined effects of the larger systemic changes and the new institutional dynamics were not fully established by the middle of 1995, and it is little more than speculation whether these changes will become permanent or be reversed. If the changes continue, however, the House of Representatives will be a different institution operating in an era of American government quite unlike its recent "post-reform" experience. That new system will in some ways be more as the Founding Fathers intended, with a limited national agenda and vigorous states, and a greater balance between a more ascendant Congress and a relimited president. On the other hand, the Founders would likely be alarmed by the personalization of power in both the legislative and executive branches of the national government with legislative issues distilled down to personal disputes between the president and the Speaker.

Conclusion

The shift toward high-profile aggressive conservatism in the House Republican party is important, and has implications in many areas of congressional research, including the role of congressional parties, interbranch relations, strategic choice in congressional elections, and the establishment and maintenance of congressional norms.

The first important change is the relative policy positions of the two congressional GOP "wings" that James MacGregor Burns identified in his *Deadlock of Democracy*. Burns, looking at the New Deal era, found a "presidential" Republican wing that was moderately liberal, internationalist, and found in the Northeast and Mid-Atlantic. There was also a conservative, isolationist and parochial "congressional" wing with geographic roots in the Midwest and Plains. The moderate wing had fewer adherents in Congress, but a moderate appeal was essential to Republicans as a base-broadening mechanism to be competitive at the presidential level.

Burns's model of two "wings" in each party retains its utility, even though aspects of the model need to be updated. The first needed adjustment is to reverse the ideological tenor of the Republican party's presidential wing in the wake of Richard Nixon's southern strategy. Conservatism, albeit in a different form than the isolationism of the 1950s, has become the dominant ideology of Republican presidents. This shift began in the 1960s with Nixon's campaign for southern Democratic votes, institutionalized as a strategy by Reagan in his three attempts for presidential office, and mimicked by Bush in his two presidential races.

The voice of moderation, on the other hand, has been narrowed to a moderate fraction of the congressional GOP. Local Republican parties, congressional representatives, and candidates in major portions of the Northeast, Mid-Atlantic and Midwest have become increasingly out of step with national Republican politics. Republican representatives from these regions must practice the politics of localism, distancing themselves from national Republican ideas, to retain their seats in the House. The decline of policy-oriented moderates and constituency-oriented conservatives, along with the rise of policy-oriented conservatives, are all partly the result of the shift in the ideological orientation of the presidential wing of the Republican party.

This changed Republican presidential strategy explains some of the factional shifts. More conservative and more ideological individuals ran for Congress. In addition, the shift in the ideological strategy at the presidential level created greater unity, at least during Reagan's two terms, between the preponderant ideology of the congressional and presidential wings. It may be that the newly responsible and conservative House GOP will require a return to moderation at the presidential campaign level if the hope of united GOP control of the national government is to be finally realized.

A second dimension of Republican "responsibility" demands a second modification of Burns's model. Burns believed that the fundamental split between the wings of the party was a general conservatism on all policy issues opposing a general moderation. Increasingly, however, disputes between the wings of the GOP were not over ideology but over which areas of policy to emphasize, bringing to mind Reiter's distinction between "regular" and "realigner" groups. Republican presidents focused on defense and foreign policy, while most congressional Republicans have attended to local needs and slightly broader fiscal issues like taxes and spending.

Disputes over which issues to emphasize were tied to the incomplete Republican realignment in national politics that occurred during the Reagan-Bush period, and is related to the perceived effects of Ronald Reagan on congressional GOP fortunes. House members may have different interpretations, depending on their own electoral fortunes. These differing interpretations are also connected to the relative fortunes of each faction. The election of a conservative Republican president who emphasized foreign policy and domestic moral issues reflected the view of the Moralist House faction and added to their numbers. Moralist ascendancy was especially prominent in the early years of the Reagan era, when hopes for Republican realignment were high. But the moralistic social agenda, although it helped Moralists, failed to bring a GOP majority in the 1980 and 1984 Republican presidential landslides. This failure of a "trickle-down" GOP realignment with a Moralist issue agenda became increasing clear to House Republicans as the Reagan-Bush era came to an end.[38]

Gingrich's pledge to create a more responsible and creative domestic agenda within the House GOP was intended as a new strategy for a majority-building effort, a modification and addition, if not a direct repudiation, of the moralistic social agenda. Now that Moralists hold a plurality of power in the conference, the party may again return to a strategy of questionable prior success.

Greater congressional party responsibility within the House Republican conference came after Gingrich became Whip, and accelerated after he was joined in the leadership by Dick Armey and others. In debate during the 1989 Whip race, moderate factions such as Patricians, Moderates, and Provincials recalled that their electoral fortunes worsened with the social conservatism of the Reagan era. In earlier times, policy-oriented Patricians and Moderates would normally advocate a return to the bipartisan policymaking that faction members practiced to their benefit before the Reagan era. That option, however, became increasingly unrealistic because of the perceived strong partisan behavior of the House Democratic leadership. Resentment over Democratic tactics made policy-oriented GOP moderates and liberals more receptive to confrontational politics.

Evidence of this is found in the dynamics of the 1989 Whip race. First, the strategy was explicitly promoted by Gingrich and his followers. Many members believed Gingrich's pledge of broad-based activism and supported him because of this appeal. For example, former representative Claudine Schneider of Rhode Island, the most liberal House Republican in the 101st Congress as measured by the *National Journal*, was a strong Gingrich supporter. She justified her position by an attack on the Democratic majority, "we were sending a signal [by electing Gingrich]. Basically there is an abuse of power by the Democrats in the House—staff allotment for committees is a joke, for example. Newt will fight for changes."[39] The policy implications of Gingrich's win were summarized by his chief lieutenant, Vin Weber, who after the victory expressed the hope that "House Republicans can lead the [Bush] White House, [which] will look to Congress for leadership on that whole second tier of issues that make up the domestic agenda."[40]

As the shifting factional representation presented here shows, conservative economic policy themes could have been predicted to be at the center of any realignment strategy organized by Gingrich. The conservative economics of the Enterprisers, however, needed the conservative cultural agenda of Moralists to unify the activist conservatives. The final piece of the puzzle was to attract enough activist Moderates spurned by Democratic partisanship. This unification of hostile GOP factions in the November 1994 elections paved the way for the takeover of the House, a House until that time extremely hostile to members of the minority Republicans. This hostility, now unleashed in rapid institutional and policy changes, may shape the House and the national agenda for years to come. Fissures among House Republicans are likely to continue, and disputes over economic, social and reform issues will frame the basic divisions in the conference. The question remains open what Republicans will decide on these issues and what will be the electoral consequences, both for Republicans in the House and in other offices. To see this internal factionalism and watch it shape politics and policy is an exciting opportunity for political science.

Notes

1. For a discussion of some of the electoral difficulties of this shift, see Rhodes Cook, "GOP Chutes and Ladders: Up in Dixie, Down in West," *Congressional Quarterly Weekly Report* 51 (12 June 1993): 1522.

2. To be sure, Vin Weber of Minnesota, Bill McCollum of Florida, and Duncan Hunter of California had all held lower-ranking leadership positions earlier. But each of these were considered "safe" aggressive conservatives who acted mostly as bridges between the old guard and the more active younger members.

3. Phil Kuntz, "GOP Moderates Take A Hit in Caucus Elections," *Congressional Quarterly Weekly Report* 50 (12 Decemer 1992): 3781.

4. Richard E. Cohen, "Capitol Hill Update," *National Journal* (12 December 1992): 2844.

5. "Armey Will Run For Lewis' Post," *Congressional Quarterly Weekly Report* 50 (6 June 1992): 1587.

6. Beth Donovan, "Freshmen Throw Weight Around, Make Their Parties Listen," *Congressional Quarterly Weekly Report* 50 (12 December 1992): 3794.

7. Donovan, 3794.

8. Alan Freedman, "An 'Uppity Minority Guy' Takes Charge," *National Journal* 25 (16 January 1993): 148.

9. Richard E. Cohen, "Capitol Hill Watch," *National Journal* 25 (10 April 1993): 880.

10. In early 1993, the conference began putting out "quarterly reports" outlining the services it has offered to House Republicans.

11. Chuck Alston, "Political Winds Blow Erratically in Clinton's Shakedown Cruise," *Congressional Quarterly Weekly Report* 51 (24 April 1993): 998.

12. James A. Barnes, "Faction Fight," *National Journal* 24 (19 December 1992): 2890–91.

13. Edward Chester, "Is the 'All Politics is Local' Myth True? The 1982 House Races as a Case Study," *Journal of Social, Political and Economic Studies* 14 (Spring 1989): 113.

14. John R. Petrocik, "Divided Government: Is It All In the Campaigns?" in *The Politics of Divided Government*, eds. Gary W. Cox and Samuel Kernell (Boulder, Colo.: Westview, 1991), 30.

15. Republican National Committee, "Contract With America" briefing book (September 1994).

16. Frank Luntz, "Public Reaction to 'The Contract,' " memorandum to Republican leaders, September 2, 1994.

17. Richard K. Armey, Christopher Shays, and Jennifer Dunn, "It's Long Enough: The Decline of Popular Government Under Forty Years of Single Party Control of the U.S. House of Representatives," (Washington, D.C.: by the office of Richard K. Armey, August 1994).

18. Ralph Z. Hallow, "Some on Right Hit GOP Contract," *Washington Times*, 28 September 1994, A1.

19. Eric Pianin, "Some in GOP Don't Buy the 'Contract,' " *Washington Post*, 30 September 1994, A15.

20. Dan Balz, "The Whip Who Would be Speaker," *Washington Post*, 20 October 1994, A1.

21. Ann Devroy, "Memo Outlines Fiscal Options For President," *Washington Post*, 23 October 1994, A1.

22. David S. Cloud, "GOP, to Its Own Great Delight, Enacts House Rules Changes," *Congressional Quarterly Weekly Report* 53 (27 January 1995): 13–15.

23. Alissa J. Rubin, "Tax Cuts Cruise to House Floor, But Face Dissent Within GOP," *Congressional Quarterly Weekly Report* 53 (18 March 1995): 799–800.

24. David Maraniss and Michael Weisskopf, "Coaxing House GOP Factions to Toe the Budget Line," *Washington Post*, 26 May 1995, A1, 20.

25. Gabriel Kahn, "In Intramural Skirmish, the GOP Moderates' 'Tuesday Lunch Bunch' Wins First Big Victory," *Roll Call*, 16 March 1995, 12.

26. David Grann, "GOP Newcomers Plan Family Caucus," *The Hill*, 12 April 1995, 3.

27. George Archibald, "$10.6 Million Saved by GOP Staff Cuts," *Washington Times*, 29 May 1995, A10.

28. Mary Jacoby, "Three-Quarters 'Open' or Two-thirds 'Closed'? Parties Can't Agree on How to Define Rules," *Roll Call*, 13 April 1995, 7.

29. Ronald Peters, *The American Speakership: The Office in Historical Perspective* (Baltimore: Johns Hopkins, 1990), passim.

30. David S. Cloud, "Speaker Wants His Platform To Rival the Presidency," *Congressional Quarterly Weekly Report* 53 (4 February 1995): 331–35.

31. Jennifer Senior, "Gingrich Immerses Self in Key Committees," *The Hill*, 1 March 1995, 3.; David S. Cloud, "Gingrich Clears the Path For Republican Advance," *Congressional Quarterly Weekly Report* 52 (19 November 1994): 3319–23; and Janet Hook, "House Republicans Rehearse Taking Reins of Power," *Congressional Quarterly Weekly Report* 52 (17 December 1994): 3547.

32. David S. Cloud, "GOP's House-Cleaning Sweep Changes Rules, Cuts Groups," *Congressional Quarterly Weekly Report* 52 (10 December 1994): 3487–89.

33. Jonathan D. Salant, "New Chairmen Swing to Right; Freshmen Get Choice Posts," *Congressional Quarterly Weekly Report* 52 (10 December 1994): 3493–94.

34. Deborah Kalb, "Government by Task Force: The Gingrich Model," *The Hill*, 22 February 1995, 3; Deborah Kalb, "The Official Gingrich Task Force List," *The Hill*, 29 March 1995, 8; and Julie Elperin, "Glut of House GOP Task Forces Creates Jurisdictional Confusion," *Roll Call*, 3 April 1995, 14.

35. Kenneth J. Cooper, "Drawing Plans for a New House; Gingrich Names 10-Member Transition Panel of Mostly Junior Members," *Washington Post*, 11 November 1995, A29; and Richard E. Cohen, "Team Gingrich," *National Journal* 27 (14 January 1995): 66–79.

36. This management style has remarkable parallels to the presidential management style of the Speaker's hero, Franklin Delano Roosevelt. This parallel was first pointed out to me by David Broder, to whom the credit for the insight is due. It is described at length in James MacGregor Burns, *Roosevelt, the Lion and the Fox* (New York: Harcourt, Brace, 1956), and Richard Tanner Johnson, *Managing the White House* (New York: Harper and Row, 1974).

37. Richard E. Cohen, "The Transformers, *National Journal* 27 (4 March 1995): 528–32.

38. Richard E. Cohen, "Despite His Landslide 1984 Win, Reagan Trailed House Winners in Most Districts," *National Journal* 17 (20 April 1985): 854–59; and Bill Whalen, "National Republican Leaders Cut Some Slack on Party Line," *Insight*, 26 March 1990, 18–20.

39. Myra MacPherson, "Newt Gingrich: Point Man in a House Divided," *Washington Post*, 12 June 1989, C9.

40. Fred Barnes, "Newtered," *New Republic*, 24 April 1989, 9.

Appendix

The model built for this analysis considers two types of member behaviors—voting behavior on roll-call votes on the House floor, and congressional activity on and off the House floor. This appendix describes the sources of the data and the methods used on the data to put House Republicans into factions.

Voting Data

The major source of voting statistics are those that have been compiled by the staff of the *National Journal* (*NJ*) since the beginning of the 97th Congress in January 1981. Each year since 1981, the *National Journal* staff has compiled ratings for every member of Congress on three ranges of policy—social, foreign, and economic policy. Annual House ratings in each category have been based on from thirty-nine to fifty-eight votes. The selection of votes is determined by journal staff in consultation with special interest groups and other organizations that rank members of Congress. A member's relative liberalism or conservatism in each area is compiled and compared against other members of Congress. Each member attains a score in each policy area on two zero-to-one-hundred scales, one measuring conservatism at zero and liberalism at 100, and the other with the opposite values. This study uses the scale with conservatism set at zero. *National Journal* scores are based on a member's comparison with other members; that is, a representative with a 28 score on the economic spectrum was comparably more liberal than only 28 percent of the House and more conservative than about 72 percent of the House. Often the two scores will not add to 100, since there may be many members

163

"tied" on the scale. The results of the analysis are printed each year in an issue of the *National Journal*.[1] This study assigns each House Republican, for each Congress since 1981, a mean *NJ* score and scores in each issue area. These scores are themselves the average scores achieved by each representative over his or her service in each Congress, almost always two scores, one from each session.

Spending propensity data from the National Taxpayers Union (NTU) are used here to complement the *NJ* voting studies. NTU publishes a "Congressional Spending Study" each year, and each study reviews every vote on congressional spending. In a typical year, approximately two hundred votes qualify for inclusion. According to NTU, it "has analyzed *every* vote that affects the amount of federal spending. By including *every* vote concerning federal spending, NTU's analysis gives a truly unbiased picture of congressional spending attitudes."[2] Some of the NTU votes are "key" votes and weighted to count more in the overall NTU score. Because it includes votes from all policy areas, NTU's score can be considered a rough estimate of support or opposition to expanding the size of government in general. But because there are fewer House floor votes on military and foreign aid spending than votes on domestic spending, members supporting defense spending may have higher NTU scores if they consistently vote against domestic spending measures than members with equal numbers of votes against spending bills in other areas, such as defense spending. As a result, the NTU score is a better measure of opposition to domestic spending (a traditionally conservative position) than opposition to all spending (a more "libertarian" position).

Activity Data

Activity data are used to indicate whether particular members or factions are interested in national policy making or local constituency concerns. Wide-ranging data on member participation are gathered from diverse sources. The largest amount of such data is gathered on individual caucus, committee, and legislative memberships. Caucus and committee data are gathered from the *Congressional Yellow Book*, a common and widely used reference for information on Congress. The data used in this study are gleaned from two basic "sweeps" of the *Congressional Yellow Book*,[3] most importantly the spring 1989 edition which was current at the time of the Madigan-Gingrich Whip race and the fall 1994 edition to collect data on Republicans in the most recent congresses. Other editions of the *Yellow Book* are used (usually the editions in the fall of even-numbered years) only if member data is not collected in those two "sweeps." Members who would fall into this special category include those whose tenure did not include 1989 and 1994, which is about 10 percent of all members.

The caucus data are divided into two basic caucus categories—national and local. The national caucuses conform closely to Susan Webb Hammond's party, personal interest, and national constituency caucuses. The local caucuses conform closely to her regional, state/district, and state/district/industry divisions. The number of each member's memberships in each category are counted, and each member is assigned three scores—a local caucus score, a national caucus score, and a total caucus score.

The committee membership data are collected from the same sources as the caucus data. Three categories of committees are employed—policy, influence, and constituency. These categories are almost identical to those described by Smith and Deering, with the modifications as described in the text. Members are assigned a number equal to the number of committee memberships they have in each committee type.

The legislative activity measure is a ratio. The number of each Republican's bill sponsorships, floor amendment sponsorships, and bill cosponsorships are used to compile a legislative activity index.[4] For each Congress, a count is made of the typical Republican's bill sponsorships, cosponsorships, and authored floor amendments by summing all such information for all House Republicans, and then dividing by the number of Republican representatives. Sponsored bills and offered floor amendments are worth five points in the scale; cosponsored bills are given one point each. A legislative activity ratio for each House Republican member is then calculated as the ratio of the personal score to the typical House GOP score, which is set at 1.0. This ratio is determined for each member for each Congress. But each member has a single ratio in his or her career, the average of the ratios he or she achieved in each Congress.

The national activity measure gives weight to participation in policy and influence standing committees, policy-oriented party committees, intraparty caucuses, and issue-based national caucuses, with one point for each representative's participation in each group. The national activity score is the sum of the incidences of involvement.

Methods

Both the voting and the activity data are used to divide members into factions. The first division is by voting data. All members with mean *NJ* scores of zero up to and including 15 are put in the "conservative" pool. Members with scores above 15 up to and including 30 are put in a "centrist" pool; members above 30 up to and including 50 are temporarily "moderates." Those with scores above 50 are put automatically in the Patrician faction.

The dividing points on the voting scale are not arbitrary. Generally, Republicans in each congress had an overall *NJ* mean in the low twenties. In addition, the typical standard deviation among mean scores was about seven. Thus, its seems that 15 and 30, approximately one standard deviation above and below the mean, are good dividing points among the archconservatives, centrists, and moderately liberal members of the party. Those few Republicans in the more liberal half of the entire House seem to deserve their own category.

The activity data is used to make further distinctions among factions. This sorting process is more complex, and the precise points to make the divisions are informed by a more personal knowledge about many of the members of the House Republican Conference and their individual friends and associates.

In the "conservative" pool, members with national activity scores less than four, plus legislative activity scores less than 0.75, are put in the Stalwart faction. Next, the remaining members with *NJ* social policy scores less than 10 and national activity scores less than seven, are put in the Moralist faction. The remainder of members in this pool are of two kinds—those with very high national activity plus extreme conservatism, or those with moderately high activity with less conservatism. All are placed in the Enterpriser faction.

In the "centrist" pool, those members with fiscal conservatism ratios less than or equal to 2.0 together with NTU scores less than 66.67 are put in the Provincial faction. All others in the centrist pool are added to the other Stalwarts selected from the conservative pool.

In the "moderate" pool, those with national activity scores equal to or greater than five are put in the Moderate faction. The remainder are placed in the Placeholder faction.

Notes

1. The studies were published in, "Rating Congress—A Guide to Separating the Liberals from the Conservatives," *National Journal* 14 (8 May 1982):

800–810; "Party Unity on Tax, Spending Issues—Less in House, More in Senate in 1982," *National Journal* 15 (7 May 1983): 936–52; "Democrats, Republicans Move Further Apart on Most Issues in 1983 Session," *National Journal* 16 (12 May 1984): 904–20; "Politics of the '80s Widens the Gap Between the Two Parties," *National Journal* 17 (1 June 1985): 1268–82; "A Year of Continuity," *National Journal* 18 (17 May 1986): 1162–91; "Moving to the Center," *National Journal* 19 (3 March 1987): 672–701; "Shift to the Left," *National Journal* 20 (2 April 1988): 873–99; "Slim Pickings," *National Journal* 21 (28 January 1989): 203–31; "The More Things Change. . . ," *National Journal* 22 (27 January 1990): 195–221; "Partisan Patterns," *National Journal* 23 (19 January 1991): 134–61; "Partisan Polarization," *National Journal* 24 (18 January 1992): 132–55; "The Great Divide," *National Journal* 25 (30 January 1993): 258–84; "Choosing Sides," *National Journal* 26 (22 January 1994): 170–89; and "Epitaph for an Era," *National Journal* 27 (14 January 1995): 83–105. Either Richard E. Cohen, William Schneider, or both authors jointly, authored each article.

2. National Taxpayers Union, *The National Taxpayers Union Rates Congress* (Washington, D.C.: National Taxpayers Union, various years). The NTU issued spending scorecards for each session of each Congress through the period. Data from these scorecards was compiled and treated in the same manner as the other voting data.

3. Jodie Scheiber, ed., *Congressional Yellow Book: A Directory of Members of Congress, Including Their Committees and Key Staff Aides* (Washington: Monitor Publishing, various editions). All biographical information in the *Yellow Book* is provided by member offices. From one perspective, this is a disadvantage to objective analysis because some caucus, intraparty group, or other memberships may be excluded because the member does not wish to make public his or her participation. But the source of data can also be seen as an advantage because each office can portray its member's activities as it sees fit.

4. U.S. Library of Congress, Congressional Research Service SCORPIO Bill Digest Files (C103, C102, C101, C100, CG99, CG98, CG97, CG96), Washington, D.C.

Bibliography

Alford, John R., and David W. Brady. "Personal and Partisan Advantage in U.S. Congressional Elections." In *Congress Reconsidered*, 5th ed., ed. Lawrence C. Dodd and Bruce I. Oppenheimer. Washington, D.C.: Congressional Quarterly Press, 1994.

Alston, Chuck. "Political Winds Blow Erratically in Clinton's Shakedown Cruise." *Congressional Quarterly Weekly Report* 51 (24 April 1993): 998.

Archibald, George. "$10.6 Million Saved by GOP Staff Cuts." *Washington Times*, 29 May 1995, A10.

Armey, Richard K., Christopher Shays, and Jennifer Dunn. "It's Long Enough: The Decline of Popular Government Under Forty Years of Single Party Control of the U.S. House of Representatives." Washington, D.C.: August 1994.

"Armey Will Run For Lewis' Post." *Congressional Quarterly Weekly Report* 50 (6 June 1992): 1587.

Bach, Stanley, and Steven S. Smith. *Managing Uncertainty in the House of Representatives*. Washington, D.C.: Brookings Institution, 1988.

Balz, Dan. "The Whip Who Would be Speaker." *Washington Post*, 20 October 1994, A1.

Barnes, Fred. "Newtered." *New Republic*, 24 April 1989, 8–10.

Barnes, James. "Faction Fight." *National Journal* 24 (19 December 1992): 2890–91.

Barone, Michael, and Grant Ujifusa. *Almanac of American Politics 1986*. Washington, D.C.: National Journal, 1985.

———. *Almanac of American Politics 1990*. Washington: National Journal, 1989.

Bender, David L. *The Political Spectrum*. 2d ed. St. Paul, Minn.: Greenhaven Press, 1986.

Benenson, Bob. "Clinton Keeps Southern Wing on His Team in 1993." *Congressional Quarterly Weekly Report* 51 (18 December 1993): 3435–38.

Borger, Gloria. "Dennis the Menace Comes in From the Cold." *U.S. News and World Report*, 27 March 1989, 25.

Brooks, Warren. "Georgia Gnat With a Whip?" *Washington Times*, 17 March 1989, F4.

Brownstein, Ronald. "Yuppies and Evangelicals: The Shaky GOP Coalition." *Nation*, 15 March 1986, 301–2, 306.

Burger, Timothy J. " 'Far Right' Wins GOP Leadership Positions." *Roll Call*, 10 December 1992, 12.

Burns, James MacGregor. *The Deadlock of Democracy*. Englewood Cliffs, N.J.: Prentice-Hall, 1963; Spectrum Books, 1967.

———. *Roosevelt, the Lion and the Fox*. New York: Harcourt, Brace, 1956.

Camia, Catalina. "Some Republican Contests May Hinge on Freshmen." *Congressional Quarterly Weekly Report* 52 (19 November 1994): 3329.

Chester, Edward. "Is the 'All Politics is Local' Myth True The 1982 House Races as a Case Study." *Journal of Social, Political and Economic Studies* 14 (Spring 1989): 113.

Clausen, Aage R., and Clyde Wilcox. "Policy Partisanship In Legislative Leadership Recruitment and Behavior." *Legislative Studies Quarterly* 12 (1987): 243–63.

Cloud, David S. "Gingrich Clears the Path For Republican Advance." *Congressional Quarterly Weekly Report* 52 (19 November 1994): 3319–23.

———. "GOP, to Its Own Great Delight, Enacts House Rules Changes." *Congressional Quarterly Weekly Report* 53 (27 January 1995): 13–15.

———. "GOP's House-Cleaning Sweep Change Rules, Cuts Groups." *Congressional Quarterly Weekly Report* 52 (10 December 1994): 3487–89.

———. "Speaker Wants His Platform To Rival the Presidency." *Congressional Quarterly Weekly Report* 53 (4 February 1995): 331–35.

Cohen, Richard E. "Capitol Hill Update." *National Journal* 24 (12 December 1992): 2844.

———. "Capitol Hill Watch." *National Journal* 25 (10 April 1993): 880.

———. "Despite His Landslide 1984 Win, Reagan Trailed House Winners in Most Districts." *National Journal* 17 (20 April 1985): 854–59.

———. "Gingrich: Don't Expect 'Kinder, Gentler' Politics." *Los Angeles Times*, 2 April 1989, V3.

———. "Gingrich: From Gadfly to Whip." *National Journal* 21 (25 March 1989): 743–44.

———. "Rating Congress—A Guide to Separating the Liberals from the Conservatives." *National Journal* 14 (8 May 1982): 800–810.

———. "Team Gingrich." *National Journal* 27 (14 January 1995): 66–79.

———. "The Transformers." *National Journal* 27 (4 March 1995): 528–32.

Cohen, Richard E., and William Schneider. "Choosing Sides." *National Journal* 26 (22 January 1994): 170–89.

———. "Epitaph for an Era." *National Journal* 27 (14 January 1995): 83–105.

———. "The Great Divide." *National Journal* 25 (30 January 1993): 258–84.

———. "The More Things Change . . ." *National Journal* 22 (27 January 1990): 195–221.

————. "Moving to the Center." *National Journal* 19 (3 March 1987): 672–701.

————. "Partisan Patterns," *National Journal* 23 (19 January 1991): 134–61.

————. "Partisan Polarization." *National Journal* 24 (18 January 1992): 132–55.

————. "Shift to the Left." *National Journal* 20 (2 April 1988): 873–99.

————. "Slim Pickings." *National Journal* 21 (28 January 1989): 203–31.

Connelly, William F. Jr. and John J. Pitney, Jr. *Congress' Permanent Minority?: Republicans in the U.S. House.* Lanham, Md.: Rowman & Littlefield, 1994.

"The Conservative Opportunity Society: New Directions, New Leaders for the GOP?" *Conservative Digest*, August 1984, 4–20, 37.

Cook, Rhodes. "GOP Chutes and Ladders: Up in Dixie, Down in West." *Congressional Quarterly Weekly Report* 51 (12 June 1993): 1522.

Cooper, Kenneth J. "Drawing Plans for a New House: Gingrich Names 10-Member Transition Panel of Mostly Junior Members." *Washington Post*, 11 November 1995. A29.

Cowan, Richard. "The Money Pit." *American Politics* 3 (1988): 10–17.

Cox, Gary W., and Samuel Kernell, eds. *The Politics of Divided Government.* Boulder, Colo.: Westview Press, 1991.

Cunningham, Kitty. "With Democrat in White House, Partisanship Hits New High." *Congressional Quarterly Weekly Report* 51 (18 December 1993): 3432–34.

Davidson, Roger. *The Postreform Congress.* New York: St. Martin's Press, 1992.

————. *The Role of the Congressman.* New York: Pegasus, 1969.

Davidson, Roger, and Walter Oleszek. *Congress and Its Members.* Washington, D.C.: Congressional Quarterly Press, 1981.

————. *Congress and Its Members.* 4th ed. Washington, D.C.: Congressional Quarterly Press, 1994.

Devroy, Ann. "Memo Outlines Fiscal Options For President." *Washington Post*, 23 October 1994, A1.

Diamond, Sara. *Spiritual Warfare: The Politics of the Christian Right.* Boston: South End Press, 1989.

Dodd, Lawrence C., and Bruce I. Oppenheimer. "Consolidating Power in the House." in *Congress Reconsidered*, 4th ed. ed. Lawrence C. Dodd and Bruce I. Oppenheimer. Washington, D.C.: Congressional Quarterly Press, 1989.

Donovan, Beth. "Freshmen Throw Weight Around, Make Their Parties Listen." *Congressional Quarterly Weekly Report* 50 (12 December 1992): 3794.

Duncan, Phil, ed. *Congressional Quarterly's Politics in America 1990: The 101st Congress.* Washington, D.C.: Congressional Quarterly Press, 1989.

Elperin, Julie. "Glut of House GOP Task Forces Creates Jurisdictional Confusion." *Roll Call*, 3 April 1995, 14.

Engelberg, Stephen, and Katharine Q. Seelye. "Gingrich: Man in Spotlight and Organization in Shadow." *New York Times*, 18 December 1994, A1, 32.

Fenno, Richard F., Jr. *Congressmen in Committees.* Boston: Little, Brown, 1973.

―――. "The Internal Distribution of Influence: The House." In *Readings on Congress,* ed. Raymond E. Wolfinger. Englewood Cliffs, N.J.: Prentice-Hall, 1971.

Feulner, Edwin J., Jr. *Conservatives Stalk the House: The Story of the Republican Study Committee, 1970–1982.* Ottawa, Ill.: Green Hill Press, 1983.

Freedman, Alan. "An 'Uppity Minority Guy' Takes Charge." *National Journal* 25 (16 January 1993): 148.

Gergely, Collette. "GOP Wins Second Special Election in Two Weeks." *Congressional Quarterly Weekly Report* 52 (28 May 1994): 1410–11.

Gigot, Paul A. "Neutron Newt Could Become GOP's Coelho." *Wall Street Journal,* 17 March 1989, 18.

Gilder, George. "Why I Am Not A Neoconservative." *National Review,* March 5, 1982, 218–22.

Gottfried, Paul, and Thomas Fleming. *The Conservative Movement.* Boston: Twayne Publishers, 1988.

Grann, David. "GOP Newcomers Plan Family Caucus." *The Hill,* 12 April 1995, 3.

Gregg, John P. "After Dick Cheney's Departure: Now Who'll Lead House GOP?" *Roll Call,* 13 March 1989, 1, 14.

―――. "Gingrich, Madigan In Whip Showdown." *Roll Call,* 20 March 1989, 1, 23.

Haeberle, Steven H. "Closed Primaries and Party Support in Congress." *American Politics Quarterly* 13 (1985): 341–52.

Hallow, Ralph Z. "Some on Right Hit GOP Contract." *Washington Times,* 28 September 1994. 1.

Hammond, Susan Webb. "Congressional Caucuses in the Policy Process." In Dodd and Oppenheimer, *Congress Reconsidered,* 4th ed. Ed. Lawrence C. Dodd and Bruce I. Oppenheimer. Washington, D.C.: Congressional Quarterly Press, 1989.

Hammond, Susan Webb, Daniel P. Mullhollan, and Arthur G. Stevens. "Informal Congressional Caucuses and Agenda Setting." *Western Political Quarterly* 38 (1985): 583–605.

Hayek, Friedrich. "Why I Am Not A Conservative." In *The Political Spectrum,* 2d ed., ed. David Bender. St. Paul, Minn.: Greenhaven Press, 1986.

Herrnson, Paul S. "Do Parties Make a Difference? The Role of Party Organizations in Congressional Elections." *Journal of Politics* 48 (1986): 589–615.

Heywood, Andrew. *Political Ideologies: An Introduction.* New York: St. Martin's Press, 1992.

Hinckley, Barbara. "Congressional Leadership Selection and Support: A Comparative Analysis." *Journal of Politics* 32 (1970): 268–87.

―――. *Stability and Change in Congress.* 4th ed. New York: Harper and Row, 1988.

Hook, Janet. "Battle for Whip Pits Partisans Against Party Pragmatists." *Congressional Quarterly Weekly Report* 47 (18 March 1989): 563–65.

———. "Gingrich's Selection as Whip Reflects GOP Discontent." *Congressional Quarterly Weekly Report* 47 (25 March 1989): 625–27.

———. "House GOP: Plight of a Permanent Minority." *Congressional Quarterly Weekly Report* 44 (21 June 1986): 1393–96.

———. "House Republicans Rehearse Taking Reins of Power." *Congressional Quarterly Weekly Report* 52 (17 December 1994): 3547.

Jacoby, Mary. "Three-quarters 'Open' or Two-thirds 'Closed'? Parties Can't Agree on How to Define Rules." *Roll Call*, 13 April 1995, 7.

Johnson, Richard Tanner. *Managing the White House*. New York: Harper and Row, 1974.

Jones, Charles O. *The Minority Party in Congress*. Boston: Little, Brown, 1970.

———. *Party and Policy-Making: The House Republican Policy Committee*. New Brunswick, N.J.: Rutgers University Press, 1965.

Kahn, Gabriel. "In Intramural Skirmish, the GOP Moderates' 'Tuesday Lunch Bunch' Wins First Big Victory." *Roll Call*, 16 March 1995, 12.

Kalb, Deborah. "Government by Task Force: The Gingrich Model." *The Hill*, 22 February 1995, 3.

———. "The Official Gingrich Task Force List." *The Hill*, 29 March 1995, 8.

Kranish, Michael. "U.S. House Faces Big Decisions on Leadership." *Boston Globe*, 21 March 1989, 1, 8.

Kristol, Irving. "American Conservatism 1945–1995." *Public Interest* 94 (Fall 1995): 80–91.

———. "Confessions of a True, Self-Confessed—Perhaps the Only—Neoconservative." *Public Opinion* 2 (1979): 50–52.

Kuntz, Phil. "GOP Moderates Take a Hit in Caucus Elections." *Congressional Quarterly Weekly Report* 50 (12 December 1992): 3781.

Lambro, Donald. "Vote for Gingrich Was Vote Against Michel." *Washington Times*, 23 March 1989, A4.

Loomis, Burdett A. "Congressional Careers and Party Leadership in the Contemporary House of Representatives." *American Journal of Political Science* 28 (1984): 180–202.

Lukacs, John. "The American Conservatives: Where They Came From and Where They are Going." *Harpers*, January 1984, 44–49.

Luntz, Frank. "Public Reaction to 'The Contract.' " Memorandum to Republican Leaders. 2 September 1994.

MacPherson, Myra. "Newt Gingrich: Point Man in a House Divided." *Washington Post*, 12 June 1989, C1, 8, 9.

Maddox, William S., and Stuart A. Lillie. *Beyond Liberal and Conservative: Reassessing the Political Spectrum*. Washington, D.C.: Cato Institute, 1984.

Malbin, Michael. "Factions and Incentives in Congress." *Public Interest* 86 (Winter 1987): 91–108.

Mann, Thomas E. "Elections and Change in Congress." In *The New Congress*, ed. Norman Ornstein. Washington, D.C.: American Enterprise Institute, 1981.

Mansfield, Harvey, Sr. "The Dispersion of Authority in Congress." In *Congress Against the Presidency*. New York: Academy of Political Science, 1975.

Maraniss, David, and Michael Weisskopf. "Coaxing House GOP Factions to Toe the Budget Line." *Washington Post*, 26 May 1995, A1, 20.

Medcalf, Linda, and Kenneth M. Dolbeare. *Neopolitics: American Political Ideas in the 1980s*. Philadelphia: Temple University Press, 1985.

National Taxpayers Union. *The National Taxpayers Union Rates Congress*. 97th, 98th, 99th, 100th, 101st, 102nd and 103rd Congresses. Washington, D.C.: National Taxpayers Union, 1983, 1985, 1987, 1989, 1991, 1993, 1995.

Nelson, Garrison. "Partisan Patterns of House Leadership Change, 1789–1977." *American Political Science Review* 71 (1977): 918–39.

Ornstein, Norman J. "Gingrich Spells Trouble for Bush." *New York Times*, 27 March 1989, A17.

———. "Minority Report." *Atlantic Monthly*, December 1985: 30, 32, 35, 36, 38.

Ornstein, Norman, Thomas Mann, and Michael Malbin, eds. *Vital Statistics on Congress, 1993–1994*. Washington, D.C.: Congressional Quarterly Press, 1994.

Peabody, Robert L. *Leadership In Congress: Stability, Succession and Change*. Boston: Little, Brown, 1976.

Peters, Ronald. *The American Speakership: The Office in Historical Perspective*. Baltimore: Johns Hopkins, 1990.

Petrocik, John R. "Divided Government: Is It All in the Campaigns?" In *The Politics of Divided Government*, ed. Gary W. Cox and Samuel Kernell. Boulder, Colo.: Westview Press, 1991.

Phillips, Don. "Reps. Madigan, Gingrich Vie for GOP Post." *Washington Post*, 16 March 1989, A6.

Phillips, Don, and Tom Kenworthy. "Gingrich Elected House GOP Whip." *Washington Post*, 23 March 1989, A1, 10.

Pianin, Eric. "Some in GOP Don't Buy the 'Contract.' " *Washington Post*, 30 September 1994. A15.

Pruden, Wesley. "Building a Fire Under the GOP." *Washington Times*, 22 March 1989, A4.

Rae, Nicol. *Decline and Fall of Liberal Republicans: 1952 to The Present*. New York: Oxford University Press, 1989.

Reichley, A. James. *Conservatives in an Age of Change: The Nixon and Ford Administrations*. Washington, D.C.: Brookings Institution, 1981.

Reiter, Howard. "Intra-Party Cleavages in the United States Today." *Western Political Quarterly* 34 (1981): 287–300.

Republican National Committee. "Contract With America" briefing book. September 1994.

Roettger, Walter B., and Hugh Winebrenner. "Politics and Political Scientists." *Public Opinion* 9 (September/October 1986): 41–44.

———. "The Voting Behavior of American Political Scientists: The 1980 Presidential Election." *Western Political Quarterly* 36 (1983): 134–48.

Rohde, David W. *Parties and Leaders in the Postreform House*. Chicago: University of Chicago Press, 1991.

Romans, Maureen Roberts. "Republican Leadership Fights on the House of Representatives: The Causes of Conflict, 1895–1931." Paper presented at the 1977 annual meeting of the American Political Science Association, Washington, D.C., 1–4 September 1977.

Rubin, Alissa J. "Tax Cuts Cruise to House Floor, But Face Dissent Within GOP." *Congressional Quarterly Weekly Report* 53 (18 March 1995): 799–800.

Salant, Johnathan D. "New Chairmen Swing to Right; Freshmen Get Choice Posts." *Congressional Quarterly Weekly Report* 52 (10 December 1994): 3493–94.

Saloma, John S., III. "Old Right? New Right? One Right." *The Nation*, 14 January 1984, 14–18.

Scheiber, Jodie, ed. *Congressional Yellow Book: a Directory of Members of Congress, Including Their Committees and Key Staff Aides*. Washington: Monitor Publishing, 1981, 1983, 1985, 1987, 1989, 1991, 1993, 1995.

Schneider, William. "Democrats, Republicans Move Further Apart on Most Issues in 1983 Session." *National Journal* 16 (12 May 1984): 904–20.

———. "Party Unity on Tax, Spending Issues—Less in House, More in Senate in 1982." *National Journal* 15 (7 May 1983): 936–52.

———. "Politics of the '80s Widens the Gap Between the Two Parties." *National Journal* 17 (1 June 1985): 1268–82.

———. "A Year of Continuity." *National Journal* 18 (17 May 1986): 1162–91.

Schneier, Edward V., and Bertram Gross. *Congress Today*. New York: St. Martin's Press, 1993.

Senior, Jennifer. "Gingrich Immerses Self in In Key Committees," *The Hill*, 1 March 1995, 3.

Shafer, Byron E. "The Notion of an Electoral Order: The Structure of Electoral Politics at the Accession of George Bush." Unpublished manuscript. Oxford University, Cambridge, 1990.

Silver, Isodore. "Neoconservatism vs. Conservatism?" *Commonweal*, 31 July 1981, 429–31.

Sinclair, Barbara. "House Majority Party Leadership in an Era of Divided Control." In *Congress Reconsidered*, 5th ed. Ed. Lawrence C. Dodd and Bruce I. Oppenheimer. Washington, D.C.: Congressional Quarterly Press, 1994.

———. "Majority Party Leadership Strategies For Coping With the New U.S. House." *Legislative Studies Quarterly* 6 (1981): 391–414.

———. "The Speaker's Task Force in the Post-Reform House of Representatives." *American Political Science Review* 75 (1981): 397–410.

Smidt, Corwin. "Evangelicals within Contemporary American Politics: Differentiating between Fundamentalist and Non-Fundamentalist Evangelicals." *Western Political Quarterly* 41 (September 1988): 601–20.

Smith, Steven S. *Call to Order: Floor Politics in the House and Senate.* Washington, D.C.: Brookings Institution, 1989.

————. "Taking It to the Floor." In *Congress Reconsidered*, 4th ed. Ed. Lawrence C. Dodd and Bruce I. Oppenheimer. Washington, D.C.: Congressional Quarterly, 1989.

Smith, Steven S., and Christopher J. Deering. *Committees in Congress*, 2d ed. Washington, D.C.: Congressional Quarterly, 1990.

Paul Starobin. "True Believer." *National Journal* 27 (7 January 1995): 8–13.

Sundquist, James. "Needed: A Political Theory for the New Era of Coalition Government." *Political Science Quarterly* 103 (Winter 1988): 613–35.

Thurber, James A. "The Impact of Party Recruitment Activity Upon Legislative Role Orientations: A Path Analysis." *Legislative Studies Quarterly* 1 (1976): 533–49.

Tiefer, Charles, and Hyde Murray. "Congressional Elites Become Take-Charge Managers in a New Era." *Legal Times*, 18 September 1982, 38–39.

Times Mirror, Inc. *The People, Press, & Politics: A Times Mirror Study of the American Electorate Conducted by the Gallup Organization.* Los Angeles: Times Mirror, Inc., September 1987.

Toner, Robin. "GOP Focuses on Cheney Succession." *New York Times*, 14 March 1989, B7.

————. "Race for Whip: Hyperspeed vs. Slow Motion." *New York Times*, 22 March 1989, A22.

Toward A More Responsible Two-Party System. New York: Rinehart & Co., 1950. First appearing as a supplement to The *American Political Science Review* 44 (September 1950).

U.S. Congress. House. Committee on Rules. "Rules Committee Calendars" and "Surveys of Activities" 95–103rd Congresses: "Notices of Actions Taken." 1994.

U.S. Congress. House. 101st Cong., 2nd sess. *Congressional Record* (29 March 1990), daily ed. H1254.

U.S. Library of Congress. Congressional Research Service. SCORPIO Bill Digest Files (C103, C102, C101, C100, CG99, CG98, CG97, CG96).

Warren, Donald I. *The Radical Center: Middle Americans and the Politics of Alienation.* South Bend: University of Notre Dame Press, 1976.

Whalen, Bill. "National Republican Leaders Cut Some Slack on Party Line." *Insight*, 26 March 1990, 18–20.

————. "Ruling the House the Wright Way." *Insight*, 6 February 1989, 24–25.

Wilson, James Q. *The Amateur Democrat.* Chicago: University of Chicago Press, 1966.

Index

About the Author

Douglas L. Koopman is assistant professor of political science at Calvin College in Grand Rapids, Michigan. He has a Ph.D. in political science from the Catholic University of America. He worked on Capitol Hill for fifteen years, from 1980 through 1995, in a wide range of personal office and committee staff positions.